FADING ADS OF
PHILADELPHIA

LAWRENCE
O'TOOLE

H

Published by The History Press
Charleston, SC 29403
www.historypress.net

FRONT COVER
One-time entrance to the Cramp Shipbuilding Machine Shop and
Turret Shop, on Richmond Street down by the Delaware River
watefront.

BACK COVER LEFT
Upper left. Detail, the Deptartment of Public Works Wagon Shop shed
in South Philly.

Upper center. A close-up of the Philadelphia Belting Company
lettering on Spring Garden Street, at the border of Callowhill and the
Northern Liberties.

Upper right. Fisherman illustration layered over (or is it under?)
lettering on the building on Market Street in Old City that was once
home to Roxy's Sporting Goods.

Bottom. "Eastern Candy Company, Home of Tas-Tee Sweets," a multi-
layered sign that used to face traffic traveling down Columbia Avenue
in Fishtown.

Unless otherwise noted, all images appear courtesy of the author.

First published 2012

Manufactured in the United States

ISBN 978.1.60949.543.5

Library of Congress CIP data applied for.

"PHILADELPHIA MANETO"

Contents

Acknowledgements

In preparing this book, I have been dependent on the help and cooperation of a good number of resources, people, institutions and organizations. Without their advice, assistance and guidance, this book would not have been possible.

I would first like to thank the staff of The History Press, who approached me with the idea of developing a book on this subject based on my blog. Without their re-energization of my interest in this endeavor, this book may have remained a long-shelved project. A special thank you to Hannah Cassilly, who provided support, encouragement and patience for an inexperienced author unfamiliar with the publishing process from a writer's perspective.

I would especially like to thank Deb and the staff at PhillyHistory.org, as well as the Greater Philadelphia GeoHistory Network, whose incredibly rich online tools, resources and general photographic and map–related help have proven to be invaluable assets in my search to uncover the history and secrets behind these faded advertisements.

I would also like to thank all the associations whose collections and resources helped inform my research and whose reference to an extent makes up a large portion of the content of this book. They include, in no particular order, the Athenaeum of Philadelphia, the Philadelphia Water Department, the Pennsylvania Historical and Museum Commission, the Institute of Museum and Library Services, the National Endowment for the Humanities, PhilaPlace.org, the Temple University and Duke University Digital Collections and the Workshop of the World website.

I would like to thank Stephen Powers, John Langdon and fellow History Press author Frank Jump for their contributions of thoughtful forewords and constructive feedback for this book.

I'd also like to take this moment to give a mention of thanks to Sandy Stewart, associate dean; Mark Willie, senior thesis advisor; and John Langdon, professor; all of whom were my teachers at the Drexel University Nesbitt College of Design Arts (now named the Antoinette Westphal College of Media Arts and Design). Their education, direction and mentorship helped shape my thesis, the forebear to this book, as well as laid the groundwork for my career in graphic design and art direction.

I would also like to thank the City of Philadelphia, the very subject of this book, for simultaneously inspiring me and frustrating me. I don't know how I managed to live here for thirty-five years, and yet it's still inconceivable that I ever left. The city has always been such a big part of who I am and how I became the person I am today, and this book has been an interesting exercise in expressing that fact.

Thank you to Linda and Lawrence O'Toole, my mother and father, who raised my sister and myself in that incredible city. Through their amazing and selfless efforts as parents, they instilled in me a creative and inquisitive nature and nurtured an instinct and desire to learn more about the world around me. They have always taken an active role in my life and provided me with the tools, education and support to pursue any and all opportunities that had come from that curiosity. I could never thank them enough.

And finally, a very special thank you to Jolene Delisle, who supported and championed this project from the very beginning. She has contributed to its success in so many ways and was a constant source of "zencouragement." Without her, none of this would have been possible.

Foreword

Faded hand-painted signs show history, extend legacy and teach technique all in one shot (and sometimes in One Shot paint). Up on Sixty-second Street, there's one such sign, a small logo painted for the Thomas Cusack Company. Thomas was a successful Chicago ad man who died in 1926, so it's probable that the logo was painted during his lifetime, more than eighty-five years ago. The serif style of the logo, the skill of its application across a four- by ten-inch area on brick and, most telling, the faded soft charcoal hue of what was once Lamp black all speak in a voice that belongs to the '20s. To be a successful enough ad man to have a skilled sign mechanic in his employ one thousand miles from the home office and to be remembered more than eighty years after his death, I'm sure he yelled a lot and paid as little as he could get away with. For all the advancements in technology, the sign game hasn't changed much since Mr. Cusack's time.

The sign game was nearly game over in the dawn of the century, but sign writing has been revived and is having a moment now. There's a resurgence in quality hand-painted work and, just as important, an affinity for that work. *Fading Ads of Philadelphia* will dress up any coffee table. This book may find its legacy in a thousand new wall signs that draw on the lessons our sign ancestors are teaching within. I know I'll do my work.

—Stephen Powers

Foreword

My career revolves around typography and lettering. One facet of that revolving crystal is my teaching typography courses at Drexel University, and Lawrence O'Toole was one of my students some number of years ago. That fact alone may have been enough for Larry to ask me to write this foreword, but he knows of my wide-ranging interest in letterforms and their history, in addition to how they attract attention and communicate ideas on the printed page.

My career began at a type shop—an advertising and graphic design industry phenomenon that no longer exists, as human beings set their own type these days in various programs on their computers. In the early 1970s, I was employed in the photo-lettering department at Armstrong Typography in Philadelphia. Photo-lettering was the process by which "display type"— type that is of a size appropriate for headlines and titles—was assembled by hand and prepared for printing. A font for use as text type is normally chosen for its easy readability, while display typefaces are frequently selected for their ability to attract attention, as well as to be read with reasonable ease.

Type shops had, and font purveyors still have, thousands of fonts from which art directors and designers choose typefaces for their work. Among the thousands available at Armstrong were a few hundred nineteenth- and early twentieth-century typefaces from the Morgan Press—a collection of ornamental fonts that are so idiosyncratic that they are inextricably linked to a time gone by. At a glance, most people would be reminded of the stereotypical "wanted poster." Douglas Morgan began collecting these fonts— mostly cut from wood, rather than metal, due to their large size—in the

1950s, when photo-lettering first arrived on the typesetting and printing horizon. Good timing, Mr. Morgan. Seduced by the distinctive styles, nostalgia and the beauty of the wood itself, I began collecting wood type in the early '70s, when it was comparatively hard to find but still relatively cheap when I did find it. Frequently, in my collecting quests, I was told, "Oh, y'shoulda been here a year or so ago. We put crates of that stuff out on the sidewalk, and it went in the trash truck." Thus, from the beginning of my career, I became acutely aware of the replacement of one technology by another.

I've noticed that there is a rather predictable pattern that occurs in the wake of technology's march. As a process that was once taken for granted becomes obsolete, there is a pause of some few-to-several years and then follows a revival of that process—no longer taken for granted but, like the water after the well has dried up, suddenly missed and appreciated like never before. We're seeing that phenomenon played out right now, as vinyl record albums are enjoying popularity not seen since the advent of audio tapes and then CDs. I can't help but imagine that when the hand-penning of books was displaced by Herr Gutenberg's invention of moveable type, few people, perhaps least of all the monks themselves, really regretted its loss for a while. The *Oxford English Dictionary* lists 1645 as the year that the word "calligraphy" was first used in print—almost two hundred years after Gutenberg initiated the use of moveable type in the western world. (The spread of new technologies, and the attendant renewal of interest in old technologies, took much longer in those days.) Centuries later, we now think of calligraphy as a very special craft, verging on being an art form. In fact, a small number of practitioners have, in recent years, broken through and now exhibit their large-scale, highly expressive, calligraphy in galleries around the world.

The wood type that survived the purge in the late '60s and early '70s has recently become highly prized. Letterpress printing, left in the accumulated dust of the late twentieth century, is blossoming anew throughout the United States, for specialty items. The wood type that shouted headlines from those presses is in great demand and has been revived and adapted for computer typesetting. There are even a handful of apps that replicate the entire process of letterpress printing—the original equipment richly photographed—and reproduced through electrons, in high resolution. Could there possibly be such a future for eight-tracks and cassettes?

Metal type was still being set upstairs from photo-lettering at Armstrong, both by hand and by Linotype machines. But in a corner of the photo-lettering department, my co-workers were experimenting with a newfangled system called photo-composition, in which the photo-typesetting was driven by a computer. In the history of typography, both of those photo-oriented systems were gone in the blink of an eye. In actuality, it was twenty years later when Apple's personal computers made their first tentative steps into creating type that was something other than crude green letters on a black screen.

So it is from this background that I began to appreciate, and soon love, the letterforms from times gone by—not only those on the printed page or the backlit screen but also wherever they may crop up. They might not crop up all that often in normal life outside the graphic design world, were it not for the wonderful, faded remains of advertisements that were painted on the sides of buildings. It is this bygone practice that is the subject of this book.

It's not easy to pinpoint the start of the Industrial Revolution—as we look back, its origins are shrouded in clouds of steam. For our purposes, let's round it off to the year 1800. Before the Industrial Revolution, virtually all type was set for books. And those books would have been primarily for the dissemination of information—historical, scientific and religious. And all type was made of metal. Also, before the nineteenth century, businesses were small and local, for the most part. Goods were created by individuals using hand tools. Shoes, for example, were made to order, one pair at a time. Accordingly, people owned no more shoes that were necessary for their lifestyle. When coal-burning, steam-driven machines began mass-producing goods, supply would have shot way ahead of demand. Demand needed to be force-fed a big dose of Miracle-Gro, metaphorically speaking. People had to be persuaded that they needed more shoes—a pair for every possible occasion in their lives. Writing a textbook to urge the purchase of more shoes would have been pretty inefficient. And so advertising was born.

Interrupting people in the midst of their daily routines to quickly inform them of the existence or benefits of a given product ("Dr. So-and-so's elixir cures all known diseases!") would be the efficient way to create demand and boost sales. These messages could best be communicated to the general population by way of handbills and broadsides. The type required for such vehicles would need to be tens or hundreds of times the size of type used to print books and would, therefore, be hundreds of times heavier. Type cut from wood was the solution.

Whenever the technology of setting type evolves to a newer stage, type becomes lighter, cheaper and faster. First lead, then wood, then photo (film and paper) and now electrons. And with each of these advances comes a spike in the public's awareness of type and the number of people becoming typesetters for the first time, and there is a concomitant proliferation of new styles. It is that impetus that gives the decorative wood types of the nineteenth and twentieth centuries their distinctive, and sometimes excessive, styles.

But the Industrial Revolution also spawned another type of type: sans serifs. Letters stripped down to their barest essence, hand in hand with another approach to demanding attention: size and weight. When type was set for books, a type family would often comprise a regular weight (which became known by the term "book"), an italic version of the same weight and a moderately bolder weight that would add gravitas to a title. With the demand for type that could stop a passerby in his or her tracks, increasingly bolder weights of many previously existing styles were created. With some of these experiments came heavier and heavier serifs. And then it must have dawned on someone that serifs create space between letters. If the serifs were eliminated, the letters could get fatter AND closer together—the latter factor allowing the overall size of the word to be greater within a given width. While the more decorative styles of the nineteenth century were too idiosyncratic to remain practical over time, sans serif types survived, evolved and thrived, and they have dominated the world of display type ever since, to the degree that they are no longer thought of as a nineteenth-century phenomenon.

Of course, the type styles that were popular for printing were put to use for hand-painted signage. In the late eighteenth and early nineteenth centuries, most businesses operated relatively locally. Communications and transportation technologies did not yet allow for national and international commerce to the degree that we know today. So where better to advertise than on the walls of the factory—and then how about that big blank wall down the street? Those bold, simply shaped, attention-getting letters are far easier to "get right" than fancy ornamental ones for one guy up on a ladder or scaffold. White, oil-based paint, with its higher lead content, is more durable than other colors. And so, it is those powerful, sans serif styles of white lettering that we see, slowly fading, on brick walls in almost every city and town in the country.

Come to think of it, why do they show up on brick walls almost to the exclusion of any other type of building? Why, it was the steam engine, of course! Steam shovels made "mining" the clay for bricks far easier and more efficient than that effort had been using human muscle and hand-held shovels. In the booming economy of the Industrial Revolution, as manufacturing demanded new and bigger buildings, brick was an ideal material—quicker and easier to stack than stone, more suitable for housing heavy machinery and more durable than wood.

Brick buildings endure. Oil-based paint with lead added resists weathering. But eventually, and very slowly, it does fade. And so, in the early years of the twenty-first century, we are left with the ghosts of a time gone by. And finally, before they have faded away completely—or the buildings have been demolished to make room for steel and glass architecture more appropriate to an electronic information-based economy—finally, we see these ghosts with fresh eyes. And with renewed reverence, we treasure our vinyl albums, homegrown produce, calligraphy, the VW Beetle and advertising on brick walls. We now see these fading words as a kind of art. We'll appreciate them now until, when they have completely disappeared from the walls, all that remains are their images in books.

One last note with regard to aesthetics: we often (but not often enough!) appreciate and enjoy the beauties that nature provides in our environment. And we glory in our triumphs over nature by way

of stunning, if prideful, design and marvel at our works. And when those monuments have outlived their purpose, we see them as decaying has-beens and then destroy and replace them with greater triumphs. But when, on occasion, we catch a glimpse of that never-ending process in mid-step, we see that we have not really triumphed at all. Nature wins. Wood rots. Paint peels, and iron rusts. Cement, brick and even stone eventually crumble. Viewed from the vantage point of human "progress," these are often seen as eyesores—to be ignored, cleaned up and gotten rid of. But when we see these processes in a moment of reflective personal witness or by way of photography, we are seeing the truth of the way of the world. Nature, on the surface, seeming always to be the same, never stops changing—itself, and everything we create. Witnessing that process and capturing it for a moment is to witness the great beauty of that great truth.

—©2012 John Langdon

Foreword

FADING ADS, NOSTALGIA AND FADING MEMORY

Fading ads are a beacon in the navigation of an urban life. These remnants of a bygone era in out-of-home (or outdoor) advertising are portals to our commercial past that inform us of our future. Not only do they illustrate the past trends of American consumerism and social attitudes, but fading ads also tell the story of the demographic shifts that have occurred in urban neighborhoods all along the Atlantic corridor, which is evidenced in ghost signs advertising long-departed goods and services in now service-poor and economically challenged neighborhoods that experienced a white flight to the suburbs in the late '60s and early '70s. Greater still, on the threshold of our perception, they are powerful signposts that not only tell us where we've been but also signal where we are going—and their sudden disappearance can elicit feelings of loss and disorientation. Fortunately, the photographic archive thoughtfully shot by Lawrence O'Toole can help aid our ever-fading memory of the past and help reorient us in our rapidly changing urban landscape.

In 1997, when I began shooting on thirty-five-millimeter chrome film what became the Fading Ad Campaign website, I had no idea the kind of interest in vintage painted wall ads that would be generated by my photo archive. Within a few years, urban archaeological bloggers around the country were documenting their neighborhoods with the same fervor I possess. The urgency that was driving me to document as many signs as I could in New York City and abroad was fueled by my grappling with mortality and an ambiguous HIV prognosis. The lens though which I saw the city and the world was shaped and polished by my own unexpected long life, which was paralleled in the unexpected long life of these "ghosts." Naturally, it was encouraging to see the work of others who shared the same affection for the written history left silently on the sides of building walls for those who cared to notice them.

O'Toole is one of those caring young documentarians who looked up to notice and document these resilient illustrations and text, knowing how tentative their existence is in an ever-changing urban landscape that has a profound influence on our exteroception. The moment you first become mindful of fading ads is a life-changing one. Once your awareness of fading ads is part of your everyday perception, you begin to see them everywhere, and where there are none, you perceive their absence as well. Sometimes you imagine you see letters on the side of a wall where there is nothing more than the uneven texture of concrete and the mottled colors of aging brick.

The disorienting effects of the disappearance of a graphic milepost that signaled you were almost home can be even more profound. As the body moves through the city, the discovery, presence and disappearance of these images possess a kind of liminal quality where the everyday ritual of going to work or returning home is anchored on these evanescent physical graphic landmarks. Their vanishing can alter your navigation. Reciprocally, in older parts of the city you may look up and begin to scan the almost imperceptible messages painted on the sides of buildings and begin to see parts of a word or a figure, then on a rainy day, the whole narrative comes to life and a century-old message is transmitted. Instantly you become aware that this is a place where people have lived; almost as if you were viewing an ancient ruined dwelling, the history of a past people is revealed. Photographing the message then extends that history by making you part of it.

In my book, *Fading Ads of New York City* (The History Press, 2011), Dr. Andrew Irving, a visual anthropologist at the University of Manchester, wrote that the moment someone photographs a fading ad,

there are at least three different registers of time at play. There is the time that is contained within the fading advertisements themselves: a kind of social and historical time that bears witness to the passing of fashions, commercial possibilities and successive years of weathering, which in some cases took place over the whole of the twentieth century. Then there is the time of the artist, that precise moment when [the photographer] *took the original photographs, the particular assemblage of light, weather and aesthetic judgment out of which the photograph emerged. As Roland Barthes writes in Camera Lucida, "Of all the objects in the world, why choose* [why photograph] *this object, this moment, rather than some other?" Lastly, there is the time of viewer who is looking at it, as if through a corridor of time, in which they are not just witnessing the world in the moment* [the photographer] *released the shutter but the history of* [the city] *that is contained in the advertisements' fading colors as seen from the present.*

We are all fortunate that Mr. O'Toole has chosen to carefully capture these moments in our time for posterity. Philadelphia is a city steeped in early American history, and O'Toole goes into great detail about the history and context of the painted sign and the advertising industry. Even before we were a nation independent from Great Britain in 1729, Benjamin Franklin first published advertisements in his *Pennsylvania Gazette* in Philadelphia, and later, in 1742, he printed the first American ads in his *General Magazine*. By the late nineteenth century, Philadelphia was a national advertising mecca with some of the largest ad campaigns in advertising history being generated by N.W. Ayer, who helped the National Biscuit Co. (N.B.C.) in 1898 launch the ubiquitous Uneeda Biscuit campaign with the classic slogan "Lest you forget, we say it yet, Uneeda Biscuit." Eventually, N.W. Ayer launched the first million-dollar advertising campaign in the early twentieth century for N.B.C., which later became Nabisco in 1971. Traces of these fading remnants can still be seen from New England to New Orleans.

In my book, I also grappled with the notion of how a feeling of nostalgia for viewers of fading ads affects how they experience them. In 1966, Pier Paolo Pasolini said, "If you know that I am an unbeliever, then you know me better than I do myself. I may be an unbeliever but I am an unbeliever who has a nostalgia for a belief." The allure of past expressions in ads runs deeper than nostalgia. It is a belief that clutching onto the familiar as we plunge into the new millennium may inform our future decisions. These ads are something we can physically touch. They are markers of the passing of time. The rate at which technology is growing elicits new forms of social development. These signs are part of us and remain closer to us in terms of time and body than our grasp of what may be coming along. The Internet can either augment or attenuate the impact of advertising and human society depending on how much more or less prominently electronic advertising and social networking become ever more intertwined with our day-to-day lives.

Gloria Steinem said on HBO's *Real Time with Bill Maher*, "Nostalgia is a form of obstructionism." It is a moot point to where we can move forward without looking back. Some individuals, communities and nations seem to progress with relative ease without looking where they've been. Others maintain the past as an ongoing reference to the present. Nonetheless, as the old forms surely fade, the new and upcoming ways of being call for new forms of adaptation. The challenge is keeping oneself ahead of the learning curve. O'Toole is an adaptive documentarian with a keen perception of the past and how to portray the past to a contemporary audience, while keeping an eye on the future. I believe O'Toole's motivation is not underpinned by a sense of nostalgia but rather a fascination of how the ways of the past have influenced us today and how these digitally preserved artifacts will influence us tomorrow. The preservation of memory is not in itself an act of nostalgia.

Recently, Professor Gerald Torres of Texas University in Austin said, "Nostalgia is corrosive and you need to banish nostalgia in my view," leading us to ask why Torres might say such a thing about the "good old days." Nostalgia is a response to the loss of discernible landmarks, within either one's external or internal landscapes. Not only can the loss of a fading ad, a familiar building, city block or perhaps even an entire neighborhood that has been transformed by "urban renewal" be devastating to one's spatial-temporal perception, but the loss of a meaningful place where one experienced personal history will also fade progressively in their memory as it physically deteriorates, as our memory is unstable right down to the level of the neural proteins, transmitters and molecules in the brain, nervous system and muscular body (Rose 2003). Equally, our ability to effectively navigate our internal schemas underpins our sense of well being and usefulness and to a large part is coupled with our ability to effectively navigate through an urban space-time. Consequently, even our so-called long-term, embodied memories enter an unstable state and undergo transformation during acts of recollection and expression before being re-patterned back into the brain and body in a new emotional context (Nader 2003; Walker et al. 2003), which is influenced by a current existential state that now is including a feeling of loss.

Furthermore, what makes nostalgia equally corrosive is if one soaks in it too long, at which point it will dissolve our determination to recognize and give significance to those new landmarks that foster growth and equilibrium toward future proprio-coherent senses of well being. Often we are anchored to our past through recollections

of a younger, more vital self, which creates a dissonance when we confront our current self. Perhaps it is wise to banish this cause of stagnation—the corrosive eating away at our tenacity to move forward in life—which is an obstruction, often manifested in anxieties over becoming outmoded. Art forms and the media on which they are recorded are also becoming outmoded. Is the art of the "wall dog" quickly drifting toward obsolescence as well?

What other forms will advertising take in the next century? Will ads be even more temporary? Will they impact the environment in monumental ways, or will they become increasingly tenuous and miniscule? Will they be projected, holographic, canyon-sized images that disappear with the flick of a switch? Will they continue to beckon us toward the things we need, the things we don't have or the things we can't do without? And will we ever again believe words like "the purest and the best"?

Much of what I learned about the history these images reveal, the companies that were being advertised, their products and the sign companies that painted them was from standing behind people who came to see my work at the New-York Historical Society from August to November 1998. I often went and listened intently on many occasions that summer as a "fly on the wall," just to see my work discussed by the crowd. It was through the NYHS that I met one of its most treasured and knowledgeable historians, Kathleen Hulser, who later came to write a brilliant epilogue for my book. In

Hulser's essay "The Collaged City," she states:

City observers perceive signs as part of a collage of sensations rather than as individual and discrete messages and objects. Imagine the city observer as a stroller—what the nineteenth-century Parisians celebrated as a flaneur—who watches the ever-changing spectacle of scurrying people against an unplanned scenography of building angles, sign fragments, windows silhouetted like movie stills and flash frames created by traffic lights. This is the visual and psychological collage that gives the old wall signs their persistent significance in the city. Thus, when we isolate rare and now precious images of wall signs, we may lose sight of the fundamental texture of how people experience them in the city.

Over time, through intense collaborations with my audience and growing with the notion of fading ads being a significant part of my everyday experience, I learned how these images tell the story of the human body and how it moves through the city's size and scale: forever propelled by desires and needs, we only need to look up to see how the story of the body is made explicit through the vast amounts of visible advertising on the city's surfaces. Indeed, what has become apparent is the relationship between people's bodies, advertising and the urban landscape over the past century.

The questions and challenges presented by the human body are a narrative that is writ large and continually played out on the surfaces of urban buildings and walls. By focusing on such signs, we are offered a glimpse into the cultural, moral and medical values of past eras. Our bodies break down, a human failure that warrants cures and preventative medicine. Our bodies have needs that sometimes get us in trouble, either by the results of excesses or the consequences of social and religious constricts. Our bodies need comfort, shelter and security. Our bodies need pleasure and sensual stimulation. Our actions to fulfill these needs also pit our bodies against conventional, social and religious mores. Ultimately, our tired bodies decay and die. All the trials, tribulations, joys and pains of the body can be mirrored in these ubiquitous signs that envelop us.

O'Toole shares the same love I have for the painted ad, both from a historical and design standpoint, and has had an equally enriching collaboration with his audience. Coincidentally, we started noticing fading ads around the same time, almost as if they were part of our collective subconscious. When I first came to notice O'Toole's Philadelphia "Ghost Sign Project" in the fall of 2007, I was excited to see him begin to get the attention he deserves. In a November 2007 *Philadelphia Inquirer* article called "Looking Up for Ghosts of Philly's Past," O'Toole's passion for urban archaeology was at last revealed to a greater public other than his blog following, which I'm sure grew as a result. A decade had passed since I had taken my first photograph of a fading ad, and I was happy to see that the tradition of urban archaeology was being

continued in the City of Brotherly Love. We cross-linked each other on our blogrolls and have been in correspondence ever since.

What I love most about O'Toole's Philadelphia Ghost Sign blog is his brilliant use of geocache location details and the pin drop on an interactive map. This clever use of Internet technology is vital in the understanding of the density of fading ads in our urban landscape and crucial to the development of tools and models that will foster their preservation, such as apps written for the iPhone or iPad for self-guided walking tours that explore extant and extinct signage and utilize global positioning technology to trigger spoken narratives, videos, music and other multimedia experiences. Since the commencement of O'Toole's photographic archive, I'm all too sure that many have faded out of existence, been covered over or destroyed. But still, many silently cling to the walls of buildings, hiding in the shadows of a northern exposure and barely noticed by the rushing passersby. With the growing awareness of these discolored portals to our past, the need for their preservation will hopefully grow in tandem. Although I'm not a believer in sign restoration (as they are, in my opinion, best left alone to fade into imperceptibility), I can understand a local municipality's desire to resurrect them. In the Netherlands, for instance, signs that are uncovered or discovered are restored to serve as a marker of what that place had once been.

Fading ads are and will always be a metaphor for survival. Resoundingly, they echo the struggle of the

producers and consumers in an ever-changing global economy. Painted by hand, they illustrate the resiliency of commercialism and the art driven by it. Gently, they remind us of who we were, who we are now and what we can be. With the welcomed addition of O'Toole's monograph in the growing catalogue of American urban archaeological studies, I know that things are looking up for fading ads as he is part of a growing culture committed to keeping these mileposts fresh in our collective memory.

—Frank H. Jump

Preface

A city's faded painted advertisements— the ghosts of a lost urban landscape— are history in plain sight. They are tangible ways to tell the histories of changing neighborhoods, industries and ways of life. The goal of this book was to capture just a few of the examples of the fading signage and advertisements in the city of Philadelphia and to include them as part of an archive intended to document and share these images. But beyond simply documenting the images, I was hoping to attach whatever interesting and relevant historical information and personal stories I could find to help place these interesting artifacts in context. It is my hope that through this work, the memory of these signs can be preserved before they are lost altogether. Whether you are a history buff, an urban archaeologist, a designer who loves lettering, a native of Philadelphia or just curious, the contents herein should help provide a unique and interesting perspective of the city through history and art.

So, you may ask yourself: how did a book like this come about? This is not a commonly discussed topic. So where would something like this come from?

I must admit, it's not something that I have been doing for a very long time, nor something that I was doing in any sort of serious fashion. At first, I didn't even know anyone else doing something like this. It was all really just a way to experiment with some interesting photographs I had taken.

The whole project actually began many, many years ago as an offshoot of the research I had been doing for my senior thesis when I was a student. I was attending Drexel University in West Philadelphia, at what was then called the Nesbitt College of Design Arts.

While I graduated with a degree in graphic design, I had originally applied to the architecture school at Drexel. As a matter of fact, I had applied to the architecture programs at almost all colleges to which I applied. I thought at the time that architecture would be my calling. I had worked for a number of summers, both as an intern and then later as a part-time employee, at Vitetta Group. Vitetta is a well-known architectural firm in Philadelphia that specializes in historic preservation and the new construction of schools. Despite being interested in architecture, I found myself being placed into the marketing department at the company. I had some knowledge of page layout applications on Apple Macintosh computers, and it just so happened that the company had just purchased a few brand-new units for the department. This was my first taste of what it would be like to work as a graphic designer, and I started to like it a bit more than the idea of working as an architect. I worked on and off at the firm well into my college years, just about up until my junior year.

One of the more interesting things about becoming a designer is learning about the history and importance of letterforms. When in school, I took numerous typography classes, studying the shapes, dimensions and strokes of letters; the way in which they are formed; and the origin and historical context of their composition. I learned about the styles of lettering and their influence both of and by culture. In addition to learning how this would affect typesetting and layout in terms of traditional graphic design, I also learned the basics of hand-lettering, the same basics employed by professional sign painters whose work I would eventually come to seek out and document. One of my professors for many of these classes was John Langdon, who contributed a foreword to this book.

Another subject that I pursued in school was photography. Black-and-white film photography, as well as the chemical processing and printing techniques, were required coursework for all design majors at Drexel. Brandishing my trusty manual Canon AL-1, which I had bought at a pawnshop for a paltry thirty dollars, I scoured Philadelphia and the surrounding environs, capturing images for school projects on the study of light and shadow. But more and more often, I started pointing my second-hand lenses toward the crumbling ruins of old manufacturing sites and industrial complexes—places like the dilapidated Wanamaker Shirt factory, formerly the National Licorice Company building, a massive warehouse that used to sit proudly at the corner of Broad Street and Washington Avenue. From these early photographs arose my interest in documenting a changing city.

All of these elements—architecture, typography and photography—would wind up playing major roles in the culmination of my studies at the university. I had spent four years studying to be a graphic designer at Drexel. When I became a senior and it came time to decide on a senior thesis subject, I thought it would be a good combination of my interests, both in a personal and academic sense, to document signage and lettering from a particular geographical area. I would then design, develop, produce and hand-assemble a book that captured the sense of that space using photographs, layout design, archival maps and text and found materials from the area itself that I would scan or photograph.

My first idea for a subject was to capture the sculptural signage of the Googie-style motels and boardwalk attractions of the beachfront resort town of Wildwood, located at the far southern tip of New Jersey. Also known as "Doo-Wop" or "populuxe" style, Googie was a form of modern architecture influenced by car culture, tiki culture and the aesthetic of the space and atomic ages. I had a strong connection to the town and its signature architecture, beautiful neon and wacky signage, having spent many of the summers of my youth there on the beaches and boardwalk. I thought using this town as a subject would be a great way to not only showcase what I had learned over the years as a Drexel design student but also to serve as a vehicle to document and preserve these signs and motel buildings at a time before there was any real effort to mark those structures as historic landmarks.

As luck would have it, just as I started to begin my research and photography scouting on the area, a strong tropical storm swept the East Coast, and many of the signs had been boarded over or taken down as a precaution against damage. Also, I had hoped to collect ephemera such as pamphlets, ticket stubs, discarded packaging and advertisements to supplement my photographs. But since most businesses shuttered, and the storm itself cleaned the city of much of the boardwalk-related tickets and scraps of paper and the like, there wasn't much to collect. So unfortunately, it seemed like Wildwood as a subject was just not going to be able to work within the timeframe I had to complete the thesis project.

So I instead turned my attention from the Jersey Shore back to Philadelphia—Old City Philadelphia, to be exact—and decided to do that same sort of documentation of a place through photographs, layout and found materials, only here in the city. It was in the course of the collection of materials in and around Old City that I began to notice the large number of mysterious eroded signs painted on the sides of older buildings. I took photos and mental notes of these signs and even incorporated a number of them into the thesis, but most of these images were simply made into film negatives and stored until after I graduated.

It's hard to pin down exactly the one thing that got me really interested in these signs. Maybe it's the idea of these remainders of past society that are hidden in plain sight, a sort of urban archaeology that one need only see to appreciate. Maybe it was the act of noticing one unexpectedly and then suddenly seeing them everywhere. It's like the opposite of that saying about "seeing the forest for the trees"—it's amazing what one finds when just looking up and focusing.

I do, however, know what event prompted me to begin the act of documenting these signs: my attention was piqued by the signage that was coming down along with the demolition of the buildings. The first of these demolitions was the Jack Frost sugar refinery complex that once stood at Delaware Avenue and Shackamaxon Street. At the time, I was more interested in the sheer size of the structures and the fact that it took so many attempts (even with explosives) to successfully bring the main constructions down. I remember getting a few photography classmates into my car and heading down to that part of Delaware Avenue to capture the last few walls coming down. Once I developed the film—actual physical black-and-white film! Developed in darkrooms! With chemicals!—I finally took notice of the letterforms painted on the exteriors of the buildings. There was nothing particularly interesting in terms of signage—just white lead paint spelling out "Shackamaxon Merchants Warehouse" in uniform slab lettering. But there was something about the fact that those words would no longer advertise the business as they had for the past eighty-some odd years that I found striking, almost moving.

So I started seeking out similar structures that were soon to be torn down. For example, the National Licorice factory at the corner of Broad Street and Washington Avenue, which was being razed to become a parking lot. The "Quaker Oats Sold Here" advertisement at Third and Mintzer Streets in the Northern Liberties, which I was able to capture just before its demolition to make way for a series of condominiums. I came to the realization that a good many of these signs were in jeopardy, as the landscape of the city, which in some neighborhoods had remained unchanged for

many decades, suddenly began to transform.

At first, I was looking at these signs and faded advertisements from a purely aesthetic standpoint. Quick, snap a photo of that cool sign before it's gone! But now I had this wealth of photography left over from the compilation of the research and documentation for my thesis, and I discovered that the most interesting of these images were the photographs of my faded advertisement findings. After reading an article in *WIRED* magazine, I decided to try my hand at the (then) relatively new art of blogging. I signed up for a Blogger account and posted photos of ads, along with what I thought the ads said and the approximate address. Later, I mapped their location via Google maps so that others could locate them—this was well before any digital cameras had such things as geotagging capabilities. And thus, the blog now known as "The Ghost Sign Project" was born. Its content would be the skeleton for what would eventually become this book.

As with any sort of hobby, a deeper curiosity started to take hold as I began investing more time with this pet project. Eventually, just simply capturing the faded letterforms and peeling paint on film (and later in pixels) was no longer enough. I wanted to know a little bit more about what it was that I had been photographing. What was the original purpose of these signs? Why were they here? What were they advertising? Who was their audience? The first driving factor, understandably, was just trying to decipher exactly what these signs said. Was that letter

an L or a D? Was that an ad for chewing gum, or bread, or perhaps both, painted and visible at different times?

There were a number of books that I found invaluable for both searching for information about signs as well as inspiration—books such as *Still Philadelphia: A Photographic History, 1890–1940,* by Miller, Vogel and Davis via the Temple University Press. But finding signs randomly in books and lining them up with signs that still exist in present-day locations was a happy accident and one that did not occur often. I needed something a bit more geographically organized and, more importantly, indexed and fully searchable. That led me to the Philadelphia City Photo Archive. The archive contains over two million city photo records that date as far back as the late 1800s. Its companion website, PhillyHistory. org, contains a growing collection of those photos, which can be searched by keyword and date and by proximity to an address, intersection, place or neighborhood. Through this resource, I was able to not only determine what many signs I found had originally said and looked like, but I was also able to mark their place in history by the age of the photograph. This helped me date the signs and better understand their context within their surroundings. I am very grateful for the support of the Institute of Museum and Library Services and the National Endowment for the Humanities, whose efforts and funds help start and maintain resources such as these.

Another tool that I found indispensable in determining when

and where in time a businesses was located was the Greater Philadelphia GeoHistory Network. Its online mapping tool, which overlays present-day street maps and points of interest on top of historical city atlases, further helped me narrow down what a sign may have been communicating and during what time period.

Once I was armed with the knowledge of what some of these signs said and was a bit clearer as to their geography, deeper questions emerged. What was the meaning and purpose behind these signs? What exactly was Kolb's Pan Dandy? Who were John Roebling and Sons, when were they in business and what did their company sell or do? The results of this search for answers led to many surprising discoveries, some of which I will be sharing in this book.

As with any project, there are always more things to do. There are more signs that I know exist but that I need to capture, and there are still so many more that are out there waiting to be rediscovered. Slowly but surely, we lose these signs to the ravages of time and, more often these days, the wrecking ball. Sadly, a good portion of the signs in my archive have already been destroyed or covered up, some of which were never fully documented properly. Even a handful featured here have been lost since I started writing this book.

So welcome to a small sampling of the world of Philadelphia's faded advertisements. I'm sure you're eager to get started. This book can be read, viewed and used in a number of ways. Start at the beginning and read through to the end, in the traditional fashion; skip to a neighborhood of your choosing and browse; open any page and explore outward from there. There is no right or wrong way to check out the contents. This book, while historical and fact-based in nature, has no hard-coded footnotes and is trying not to take itself too seriously. It is meant to be enjoyed by those who live in the city of Philadelphia and who can relate to the signs that they have seen and may see every day, never knowing their history or background. It is also meant for people everywhere around the globe who simply enjoy urban archaeology and the discovery of hidden treasures in our everyday surroundings.

So please do enjoy this book, and always keep looking up.

Introduction

A BRIEF HISTORY

The advertisement. It has become such a part of our lives that it is impossible to remember a time prior to advertising and signs in our landscape. There aren't many advertising practices that have been in use longer than that of the sign. It would seem that the history of the sign is nearly as old as the history of civilized man, spanning some five thousand years. We find imagery and words on establishments in the ruins of Roman and Greek structures. We find the inscriptions of builders and pharaohs on buildings from Egyptian antiquity. In fact, until the eighteenth century, advertising was strictly an outdoor medium. Other than word of mouth, painted wall advertising was the primary means of communicating and promoting a business, goods or services.

A BRIEF HISTORY OF SIGNS IN PHILADELPHIA

It is fitting then to discover that display advertising in Philadelphia is at least as old as, if not older than, our very nation itself. Even before printing became common practice throughout the colonies, hand-lettered signs and carved symbols were used by businesses to advertise their wares.

Illiteracy was always an issue facing the public, and during the 1600s, it was as pervasive a problem in England as it was here in the newly founded colonies. Early advertising signs were simple, pictorial and representative in nature to help alleviate this problem. Signage in England originated with public houses, or pubs, and had been mandated in the fourteenth century by the king so that ale tasters could locate drinking establishments to ensure their quality. The practice of constructing increasingly elaborate carved signs for each pub, in a sort of design one-upmanship, caught on with most other types of businesses. Soon, the sign, whether elaborate artwork or just simple lettering, became commonplace for any type of shop or service.

The practice of symbolic sign making in eighteenth-century England directly influenced early Philadelphia shop signs. Businesses brought these sign making practices with them when they came to the shores of the New World looking to establish themselves in the developing colonies. Early tradesmen used simple imagery or symbols of their trade to advertise their wares or, in some cases, simply just used the actual product itself. As observed by *Signs of the Times* magazine:

> *A basket maker hung a basket on a pole; the saddler's shop was identified with a horse head; a miniature fire engine signified a fire pump maker; a chemist shop used the unicorn's head on the signboard; a breeches maker very aptly pictured a pair of breeches on his sign; a ship outfitter used the sign of the fish; a boot maker chose a buckle shoe, and the gunsmith appropriately used a shot gun or rifle...It is not at all surprising that a lock and two keys identified a locksmith, or the spinning wheel was used by the weaver, a pretzel by the pretzel maker, the tensed arm and mallet symbolized the gold beater, and the saw for the carpenter.*

At first, painted signs on businesses were more modest and simple "fascia signs," which consisted of lettering painted in a band across the face of a building. Purely informational, they were usually located between the first and second stories of a storefront, factory or warehouse and identified the business or service contained within. This area of the façade eventually became known as the "signboard." As time and tastes progressed, these signs would grow to become quite artistic in nature as tradesmen competed for business and sign painters developed more impressive and unique ways to help their clients gain attention.

Turn-of-the-century photographs of Philadelphia storefronts on Market Street and Broad Street show buildings literally blanketed in signage and lettering advertising wares and services. Every window, every column and every flat expanse of brick was put to use—even the roofs held dimensional metal signage. It is hard to imagine these days all those images and slogans vying for the attention of the pedestrian walking down the street. It must have been something bewildering and wonderful to witness, much like seeing modern Times Square in person for the first time.

At the turn of the twentieth century, signs began to climb higher up on structures to take advantage of new technology. Better building techniques and advances in materials, such as steel, led to the possibility of taller buildings. Also, mechanization of many types of industry meant that many, such as garment manufacturing, could practice their trade in buildings within the populated city. Signs needed to rise above or around these obstacles in order to be seen. Taller buildings provided a new canvas for advertisers, and so sign painters began to move up from the simple signboards and ply their trade between the upper stories of high-rises. There were now new areas to place ads, such as those designed to be seen from elevated train tracks. Buildings became

massive handbills, meant to be read from top to bottom. Often, these painted exteriors functioned like an inventory or directory, listing all the businesses located within the building or all the services and products offered by a company.

WHAT IS A FADED ADVERTISEMENT?

So what exactly is a faded advertisement? It is a weathered, painted sign, at least fifty years old, on the exterior wall of a building, which heralds an obsolete product, an outdated trademark or a clue as to the history of a building's occupancy. In many cases with older signs, white is the only color remaining, as the white lead paint deteriorated slower than the other colored paints used in the sign making process.

Many painted signs that are still visible today date from the late 1800s through to the 1960s. While larger cities, especially those on the East Coast, featured painted advertisements from early colonial times, in most other newer urbanized cities, advertising signs such as these were most commonly brought into practice in the decades before the Great Depression.

Another common name for these signs has been "ghost signs." The term "ghost" comes about due to two phenomena. First, some faded ads can reappear on walls when the light is just right, after a rainstorm or when the viewer had observed the sign long enough to read, or rather decipher, what at first seems to be unintelligible remnants of paintbrush strokes. Second, another meaning of "ghost sign" comes

from the rediscovery of painted advertisements that were obscured or completely covered by an adjacent building and forgotten. A restoration or demolition suddenly reveals them again, in vivid color or detail, if only for a short while, with the idea that what the viewer has just seen is the equivalent of seeing a ghost.

The strict definition of "ghost sign" or "faded ad" in numerous books and articles limits them solely to signs painted on brick or stone walls. While other signs—such as neon signs, metal signs or signs painted on wooden surfaces—may be just as important in the context of history and design, these are not "faded ads" or "ghost signs" in the strictest sense, and so therefore most have not been covered by this book. Those will have to wait for another time and another work.

HOW DID THESE SIGNS COME ABOUT?

Painted wall signs could be installed and paid for in one of two ways. The first was paid for directly by the advertiser, who also owned the wall. The owner of an establishment would hire a local sign painter to install a sign on his wall to advertise his business.

The second method was to allow a national advertiser to finance the sign painting in return for a "privilege" given to the wall's owner. This "privilege" was usually a mention of the business as part of the sign. We see this most often on corner groceries or similar stores, where an advertiser for bread, milk or some other common product sold within the store would display its product and include the name of the grocer within the sign. In the years prior to billboard advertising, privilege signs were the means by which corporations could launch and sustain national advertising campaigns. In this respect, privilege signs were responsible for the rise and popularity of painted wall advertising, and this explains why they are so prolific. Their sheer number has ensured that at least a handful still manage to survive to this day, providing a unique history in the context of the modern world around them.

WHO MADE THESE SIGNS?

"Walldog" was the term used to describe the artists and sign painters who made a living painting the exterior signs and murals used as advertisements throughout the United States around the turn of the century. The term has been handed down through the sign industry for generations, and the origins are somewhat derogatory: these artists were known for working like "dogs" through the heat of the summer, bad weather and sometimes in very perilous conditions.

WHAT HAPPENED TO THE SIGN PAINTING PROFESSION?

Sign painting was, and still is, a learned craft. It is a highly specialized and difficult process. Technical skills were acquired either through vocational schools or on-the-job apprenticeships. Learning how to paint at such an incredible scale takes practice and patient mentorship. Mastering the skills of brush handling and lettering styles, as well as the techniques

of painting large-scale murals in varying weather conditions, could take many years.

In the mid-1800s, methods of advertising began to expand beyond just that of the painted wall ad. The advent of inexpensive and easily mass-produced newspapers and other printed material by mechanical means ushered in a new era for advertising, which resulted in more timely and easily reproduced campaigns. By 1889, the multi-panel billboard had been standardized in its dimensions, and national campaigns could now be easily duplicated around the country with greater speed, precision and consistency than by painting one sign at a time.

At the same time, the electric bulb—and soon afterward, the neon tube—created a whole new technology option for signage. The improvement of plastics after World War II expanded into the usage for advertising signs, making it easy to create mass-produced sign materials at low cost. All of these combined advancements, as well as the precise aesthetic afforded by mechanized production, contributed to the gradual decline of the traditional hand-painted sign industry.

While mechanization and computerization has been both a blessing and curse to the sign trade, hand lettering and sign painting is not a dead art. There has been a resurgence of interest in lettering, and a renewed interest in more humanistic approaches to letterforms in art and design over the past few years, and as such there has been renewed interest in signs and their history. As both

a designer and sign collector, I sincerely hope the trend continues.

EUROPEAN SETTLERS arrived here in the Delaware River Valley in the early seventeenth century. These settlers established small outposts that would eventually become the city of Philadelphia in the second half of the 1600s. From the very beginning of the colony, the waterfront was a vital part of everyday life in the city, and this earliest of neighborhoods became the center of commercial and residential development in the city and in the entire region. This would remain so for nearly two hundred years.

Market Street, originally called High Street, used to serve as the main artery running through the Olde City and was a direct connection from the waterfront piers and wharves to the local business storefronts and warehouses nearby. It was also the location of the High Street Market, which occupied the "islands" along the center of the street—a prime location then for advertisements. All along Market Street, signage quickly built up to publicly advertise the locations of shops and the availability and quality of goods for purchase. Although some of these signs would now be the oldest in the city, a few do survive to this day and provide a peek into the storied histories of the structures and lifestyles of this city neighborhood's past inhabitants.

RIGHT *A large but faint mural sign for two related family companies: John A. Roebling's Sons Co. and New Jersey Wire Cloth Co.*

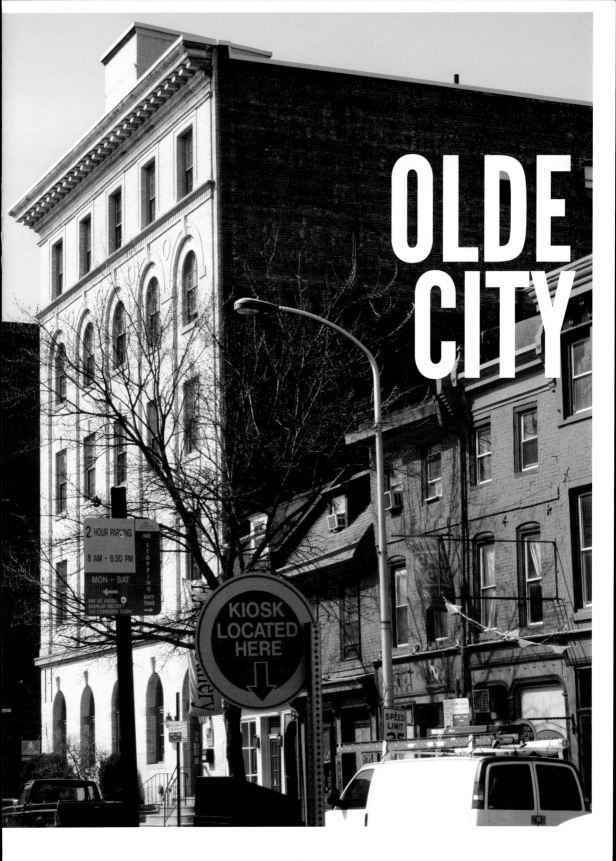

OLDE CITY

Roxy's Hunting Goods
MARKET AND LETITIA STREETS

LEFT *Painted advertisements on what was, at one time in the mid-century, Roxy's Leather Goods and Hunting Goods. Note the faint vertical lettering on the façade that faces Market Street, the large colorful main panel on Letitia and the recently uncovered lettering at street level just behind the "Franklin Ice Cream" metal sign. The current owners of the building plan to maintain the signs, and as they rehab the façade, they hope to uncover more.*

Let's start off this collection of faded advertisements with one of my favorite signs in all of Philadelphia. This is one of the signs that changed the way I looked at buildings and at cities in general and helped spark the idea of photographing and documenting signs for posterity in the first place. Once I looked up and saw this particular sign, I started seeing signs like this everywhere and started seeking out tall expanses of brick on street corners expecting (and hoping) to find more.

This incredible gem of a sign can be found at almost the very edge of the Olde City. Nearby, modern-day Interstate 95 cuts a broad swath through the neighborhood along the Delaware River and separates the city from the water's edge. At the corner of Letitia and Market Streets, the entire front façade and a good portion of the western-facing side of this stately four-story building have been covered in colorful painted advertisement. At the time it was painted, it was understandably vying for competition at the once bustling epicenter of commerce that was Market Street near the river.

The front of the building, parallel to Market Street, features white block lettering painted on the otherwise plain brick running along the vertical corner columns of the structure. The left-hand column reads "LEATHER GOODS" and the right hand column reads "HUNTING GOODS." The top portions of these words have weathered away almost completely. Some discussion with the building owner revealed that as late as the mid-1950s, there was a sporting and hunting goods supply store called Roxy's located on the premises.

But the major find is located just around the bend. Turn the corner of

Letitia Street and look up. The main side panel features a colorful three-story-tall palimpsest of slogans, illustrations and graphic devices advertising all manner of items. Most prominent is an illustrated image of a smiling fisherman, happily reeling in his first—or perhaps his biggest—catch of the day. There are many generations of signs here, their layers intermingling as they slowly weather away at different rates.

For example, a layer above (or perhaps below) the smiling fisherman illustration features the slogan "FOR QUICK RELIEF from COUGHS due to COLDS call for…" painted in a dynamic lettering style, followed by a logotype for "HOT DROPS." Interestingly, the same "Call for HOT DROPS" logotype appears toward the bottom in a different section of the sign and, due to its less prominent detail and color, perhaps was visible at an earlier time than the one at top.

In the middle section, on a background of blue, what appears to be a large hand is holding something between its pointer finger and thumb—a fishing lure of some type or perhaps a cigar—which has long since been lost to the ravages of time. Just below the image, to the right of the hand, we find a nicely embellished ten-cent price callout. Weaving throughout the sign are "LEADING BRANDS" followed by trademarks and other more generic terms like "SHOT GUNS and SHELLS," as well as "GOLF" and "TENNIS EQUIPMENT." At the very bottom of the sign is a large "LOZENGES," linked to the above "HOT DROPS." One would assume this sign to be a privilege sign, paid for in part by the advertisers depicted in the ad itself.

On the ground floor, at street level, recent removal of exterior wall paint has revealed even more lettering along

Letitia Street. It's very faint, but one can make out "Brief-cases," "Boston" and "Bags" in straightforward lettering, with numerous sweeping letters that are too faint to decipher. At the very bottom of the wall, there is a faint but ornate "MONEY" lettering treatment. This style of lettering appears to be much older than that of the above, and the fact that nothing but the white leaded paint remains supports this, as opposed to how much of the colorful paint of the large panel remains on the wall above. It would seem that at some point prior to the sporting and hunting goods business, this location dealt with transportation and shipping of luggage. Given the proximity to the river near the ferry terminal, which used to reside a handful of blocks away at the end of Market Street on Delaware Avenue, this area would make for a logical location for such a business, and the sign would be located in a prime vantage point to catch the attention of pedestrians.

Most recently the building has been undergoing restoration. This current photo shows scaffolding in place, suggesting more renovation is underway. The ground-floor storefront has been occupied for a few years now by the Franklin Fountain, which operates an ice cream and soda fountain much in the same way an establishment of its type would have done at the turn of the century. Its efforts to remove the covering paint and reveal the signs of previous tenants have helped enhance the history of the building and provide an appropriate context for its nostalgia-based business.

This sign is the first I photographed simply for its aesthetic qualities. It became part of my senior thesis at university, occupying a double-page spread at the very center of the book. Where many of the other spreads throughout the book had digital enhancements, additional artwork and effects applied to them, this spread was simply the sign, unaltered, in all its original weathered splendor.

LEFT *This is a detail of the top portion of the large, colorful Roxy's Hunting Goods mural advertisement. The happy fisherman illustration is layered over (or is it under?) lettering that reads "FOR QUICK RELIEF from COUGHS due to COLDS call for HOT DROPS."*

Wilbur Chocolate

THIRD AND NEW STREETS

It's hard to miss the sign for this one-time factory of a local chocolate maker. The building itself sits just north of the Benjamin Franklin Bridge's westbound traffic lanes as they empty vehicles traveling into the city from New Jersey. The enormous letters of "Wilbur's"—a story high and nearly a block long, thick stroked and punctuated by a period— are visible from quite a distance away. I remember always being impressed at the sheer size of the letterforms and can imagine how they must have looked when new. The sign was probably much more visible when first installed, but the lettering is now obstructed by the heights of the newer, more modern buildings toward the center of the city.

The Wilbur family chocolate company is a storied enterprise that is still in business today. In the 1860s, Henry Oscar Wilbur was successfully operating a small hardware and stove business out of Vineland, New Jersey, just across the Delaware River from the city. He and Samuel Croft, a fellow entrepreneur who owned a confectionery business in Philadelphia, decided a merger of their businesses would make good economic sense. They became partners under the name of Croft & Wilbur in 1865, starting their new joint candy business at 125 North Third Street, just south of the bridge and not very far from this location. This particular stretch of Third Street was known for the number of chocolatiers that had set up shop here. Combining the hardware manufacturing from one business with the confectionery techniques of the other, Croft & Wilbur produced molasses candy and other types of hard candies. Its main clients were the local railroad companies. These hard candies were sold to commuters riding in the passenger cars by train boys. Over the years (and in no small part due to the Wilbur business), this particular section of North Third Street became known as "Confectioner's

Row" as candy, cocoa and malt makers began setting up shop here.

The company's most popular candy, the Wilbur Bud, was introduced in 1893. The Wilbur Bud closely resembles a Hershey's Kiss but predates the introduction of that candy by almost fifteen years. This candy was produced at this facility, as in 1887, H.O. Wilbur & Sons had moved the company manufacturing to this location at the intersection of Third, New and Bread Streets.

A massive complex of brick and concrete structures, five in total, was built in different architectural styles over the forty years the business operated here. In August 1930, it was decided that manufacturing and other operations at the Philadelphia plant were to be moved outside the city to Lititz, a small town in the far suburbs of Lancaster County. The move was completed in August 1933.

What's interesting is the building's extreme proximity to the Benjamin Franklin Bridge. From the pedestrian walkway, you can almost reach out and touch the side wall of the factory—it is only a few yards away from the blue metal skeleton of the bridge.

I had always wanted to get up close to this sign by accessing the bridge's pedestrian walkways. They had been closed on and off over the years, and my visiting opportunities always seemed to conveniently coincide with those periods when the walkways weren't open. Finally, in the hopes of getting images for the book, I was able to gain access to the walkway closest to the sign; unfortunately, the opposite side walkway was closed.

Originally named the Delaware River Bridge and completed on July 1, 1926, the development and construction of the Benjamin Franklin Bridge had a direct

impact on the chocolate factory's painted wall advertising. Faux "billboards" were strategically located along the side of the building, descending along with the slope of the bridge's road surface as it heads toward the city, and were spaced out evenly between the support beams to be seen easily from a moving car. While the ads have deteriorated somewhat, and windows have been punched through the exterior wall (and the painted ads themselves), we can definitely make out the illustration of a cocoa can in one billboard, some sort of cookie or wafer-like treats in another and a chocolate bar of some sort at the final billboard.

The uninterrupted span of the brick wall was put to good use, with additional "faux billboard" ad space rented to other companies for advertising. Three of these signs are grouped at the western end of the building. Weathered badly, the first, westernmost sign has unfortunately become illegible. However, the center ad is still legible and reads, "Newton Line Co Inc. Homer NY, Fine Fishing Lines" in straightforward lettering, and the third, more ornate sign reads, "Use Lepage's Glue for Strength." The Newton Line company, manufacturers of (you guessed it) fishing line and lures, was founded in 1909 but has since shuttered. Lepage, a glue maker founded in 1876, still manufactures adhesives in Canada to this day.

A section of the building had been demolished back in the 1920s, along with the other structures in the neighborhood, to make way for construction of the new bridge. However, the company made clever use of the concrete framing left exposed by this demolition. Another ad was painted at the span's road level, completely filling the room-height void of the wall and neatly framed by the concrete pillars. This ad reads "O-Cedar, over 30 years Quality Products," along with illustrations of a bottle, a mop and other cleaning products. O-Cedar was a chemical company that began as a manufacturer of waxes and wood polishes, which were sold door-to-door by salesmen in the early 1900s. One of the main ingredients of its better-selling products was cedar leaf oil, which the company then trademarked as "O-Cedar Polish." Due to its popularity, the company decided to use the name as an umbrella for all of its cleaning products. It is still in business today, known now for its lines of mops and brooms.

LEFT *This is the same Wilbur's sign as seen from the opposite angle, looking west from the northern pedestrian walkway of the Benjamin Franklin Bridge. The lettering was painted this large in order to be seen from a great distance away; at this close range, the letters are absolutely immense. Note the period at the end of the name.*

B. Schapiro & Bro.

TROTTERS ALLEY AT THIRD STREET

LEFT *This sign sits just inside of Trotter's Alley as it passes between and through the storefronts that face North Third Street. Faded lettering reads, "B. Schapiro & Bro." with painted illustrations of what appear to be spools of thread. There may be additional illustrations of tools of some kind, but unfortunately, not much else is discernible from the sign.*

INSET RIGHT *This is a city archive photo of Trotters Alley, dated 1929, which shows the existence of signage in this spot on the inside walls of the alley passageway.* **Photo courtesy of PhillyHistory. org, a project of the Philadelphia Department of Records.**

This obscure sign is located just above a unique and interesting architectural feature. This small alley where the sign is found is typical of the way that larger blocks in Olde City began to be subdivided in the early eighteenth century.

The space behind existing row homes, in between street blocks and away from the main streets, was built up into smaller courtyards. This was in order to provide more space for residential and commercial development as the city began to grow in population. Small streets and alleys were established in order to access and service these areas. This particular passageway, a tiny pass-through named Trotters Alley, is interesting not only in the way it neatly slips between two buildings in an opening just one story high but also in that the Belgian blocks lining the passageway road surface are blue.

Belgian blocks were used as ballast for the freight ships from Europe that made the transatlantic journey to the Americas empty. The tall ships needed the weight in their hulls to keep them upright. When they arrived at the Philadelphia waterfront, the blocks were discarded, and the ships were filled with cargo to be delivered back to their ports of origin. Credit is due to a rather famous Philadelphian, Benjamin Franklin, for penning and championing a bill to use these blocks for street paving, greatly improving the quality of the public roads. Most larger and more commonly used streets have long since been repaved with the larger quarried granite setts (what most people think of mistakenly as cobblestones) and eventually, in the more modern era, with asphalt. But a handful of Philadelphia's smaller secondary and tertiary streets and alleys (like this one) still retain their older, smaller and uniquely blue-hued blocks.

On the walls of the passageway, closest to Third Street, we find a few painted advertisements. The southern-facing sign (which also faces the direction of traffic) reads, "B. SCHAPIRO & BRO." and is adorned by illustrations of what seem to be three spools of thread below the lettering. The remainder of the sign has been worn away or rubbed off from shoulder height on down. Another sign on the opposite wall reads, "DELIVERIES," with a directional arrow below.

An interesting find, of course. However, we cannot be sure of the authenticity of these particular signs, as they both may have been painted as part of a set dressing for a Hollywood movie. *Beloved* was filmed at this location in 1997, as well as others throughout Philadelphia. Archival photos do show signage here on the inside of the alleyway. However, both of these signs as they look today are clearly visible in two scenes in the movie. The location is Sethe's back-door job entrance in 1873 Cincinnati. Sethe was the character played by Oprah Winfrey. Period-correct signage, even simulated ghost signs, that are painted specifically for movies or TV shows are not all that uncommon. This may be just such a remnant from that production.

J.E. Berkowitz Mirrors and Glass

201 NORTH SECOND STREET

LEFT *The "J.E. Berkowitz Mirrors and Glass" sign, with its squared-off lettering, is slowly reappearing from behind a coat of well-weathered stucco.*

INSET RIGHT *This photo, dated 1952, clearly shows the Berkowitz sign in the upper left corner. There is a hanging sign at the street level as well. The men loading or unloading the truck have stopped to pose for the photo; it is unknown if they are delivering or picking up goods from the mirror manufacturer. Interesting to note is the sign for the Horn and Hardart (left foreground of the photo), which has now also been covered up by stucco. Perhaps someday it too will reappear.* **Photo courtesy of PhillyHistory. org, a project of the Philadelphia Department of Records.**

J.E. Berkowitz Mirrors and Glass was founded in 1920 by Jacob Berkowitz as a glass silvering business. The company originally manufactured mirrors for furniture, as well as stand-alone versions for department and variety stores from this location here on Second Street. Over the next two decades, J.E. Berkowitz became the largest silvering plant in the city and by 1940 had outgrown this facility. The outfit then moved to a larger location by the waterfront. The business continued to operate in Philadelphia until 1972, when it was moved across the Delaware River to Westville, New Jersey. The company is still in business today and is now located in Pedricktown, New Jersey.

The sign at the first location on Second Street is slowly reappearing from behind a thinning coat of stucco, and the words "J.E. Berkowitz Mirrors and Glass" in squared-off lettering are actually becoming more legible.

City archive photos help us clearly identify the sign as well. It is interesting to note there was also an advertisement for a Horn and Hardart automat restaurant here too, which was located in the building immediately next door. This sign has also been covered up by paint or stucco. The Continental Diner was constructed in the empty lot we see in front of these signs, and the present-day Continental cocktail bar has expanded into the ground floors of the buildings on either side of the diner structure. The Berkowitz Mirrors and Glass building has been vacant for decades, although it seems to be looked after and overall is in reasonably good shape. As of this writing, the grouping of buildings along this stretch of Second Street remain vacant.

KLOSFIT Petticoat

309 ARCH STREET

High up on the side of this cast-iron façade building near the corner of Third and Arch Streets, you can find a faintly visible ad for "KLOSFIT Petticoat." The ad is badly deteriorated, but we can still make out the phrase "Fits without any wrinkles" painted below. There are also the faint remnants of an illustration at left, presumably of one of the undergarments that made Klosfit a household name in the early 1900s.

The building was constructed in 1875 as the Klosfit Petticoat factory. Patented in 1907, the Klosfit petticoat is a skirt-like undergarment that differed from others of the time in that it did away with then customary and annoying drawstrings that puckered and gathered and instead made use of elastics to make for a more composed dressing appearance. In city archive images, we see that this ad space was used to advertise for other clothing companies in later years, so it would seem the building has long housed businesses associated with garment manufacture. In the 1980s, the building was renovated into condos and renamed "The Hoopskirt Factory" to reflect its original purpose.

This sign is another of my favorites. I brought *Philadelphia Inquirer* reporter Dan Rubin here to demonstrate to him the interesting nature of ghost sign spotting. He had never noticed this sign before, nor any of the others I pointed out to him during the outing before our interview. He agreed that once you see a sign such as this, hidden right there in plain sight, something from such a different era coexisting in our modern spaces, you start to see them everywhere.

LEFT *A Klosfit Petticoat ad has been painted high on the side of the factory building where these garments were once made. The tagline reads, "Fits without any wrinkles." Note also the faint remnants of an illustrated petticoat to the left of the faded lettering.*

Elder & Jenks Brushes

LAWRENCE AND VINE STREETS

For a time, this was the home of the oldest continuously operating brush and roller maker in the country, which remarkably has been making paintbrushes since 1793. I have used many of its products over the years, both for artistic and home improvement pursuits, and I still own a handful from my oil painting days back in college.

Atlases show the large factory structure appearing in the early 1900s. A signboard reading, "Elder & Jenks Brushes" is painted in large horizontal lettering across the front and side of the building, and "Brushes" has been lettered vertically on both sides of the corner of Lawrence and Vine Streets. Small signs for the current occupant, also hand painted, show that the building is being used by a footwear wholesale company.

LEFT *Painted signboard and vertical lettering on the Elder & Jenks Brushes building. The company, which was located here for a large portion of its history, continues to operate today. It has been making paintbrushes since 1793, making it the oldest company of its kind in Philadelphia and the nation.*

John A. Roebling's Sons Co.

ARCH AND BREAD STREETS

John Augustus Roebling was a German-born American civil engineer. He is famous for his wire rope suspension bridge designs—in particular, his design of New York's iconic Brooklyn Bridge. His company, founded in 1848, would also later participate in such immense projects as the Golden Gate Bridge in San Francisco and the George Washington Bridge in New York and New Jersey. He operated large wire rope– and cable-making plants in Trenton and Roebling, New Jersey.

Early in his career, Roebling offered his help in the design of the Delaware River Bridge (now Benjamin Franklin Bridge) but did not win the business. It is unknown for certain if this building at the corner of Arch and Bread Streets was an office for the Roebling business or just served as an advertisement, but the size of the ad and lack of overlapping signs suggests the former.

The Roebling advertisement is very faded and barely legible now, but by cross-referencing archival imagery of Arch Street, we can decipher some of what the ad once said. The top line reads the name of the company, which manufactured wire rope and cabling for use in those large public works projects, "John A. Roebling's Sons Co.," with other lines that read, "WIRE ROPE" and "PRODUCTS" composed below. The second part of the sign refers to the Roeblings' other business, the "NEW JERSEY WIRE CLOTH CO.," which manufactured "WIRE CLOTH and NETTING" products that were scaled for more domestic use.

John Roebling died of tetanus after suffering a foot injury on the construction site of the Brooklyn Bridge. After his passing, the company operations were assumed by his sons. After almost 126 years in business, and after the design and completion of numerous large-scale and world-renowned public projects, the company was liquidated in 1974.

Girard Estate Warehouses

20 TO 30 NORTH FRONT STREET

LEFT *This is the block of buildings on Front Street that compose the Girard Estate Warehouses. Prominently featured, although weathered, is the signage of "Robert L. Latimer Co.," the last warehouse tenant to paint its signboard. In this present-day photo, you can see repair work being done to the building. Since this photo was taken, the buildings have finished their rehabilitation; the façade has been cleaned and repainted and, unfortunately, no signage remains.*

INSET RIGHT *Here is a city archive photo of the Girard Estate Warehouses, taken in 1969, when the Latimer sign was in much better shape. The same can't be said for the buildings, as at this point, they were vacant.* **Photo courtesy of PhillyHistory.org, a project of the Philadelphia Department of Records.**

This grouping of a few warehouses along Front Street represents a final remnant of the city's commercial seafaring past and makes up a rarely found intact historic block near the Delaware River. Most of the contemporary buildings from this area were demolished during the construction of the Delaware River Bridge in the 1920s or in the construction of Interstate 95 in the 1960s, so a historically intact grouping like this exists nowhere else.

The estate of shipping magnate Stephen Girard built these warehouses in the late 1820s to early 1830s as storage space for imported goods arriving from ships at the Delaware River docks. The Robert L. Latimer & Co. whose name was last emblazoned across the signboard of these warehouses was a manufacturer and dealer of bolting cloth, mill furnishings and mill machinery.

The properties were listed on the Philadelphia Register of Historic Places in 1977, and the city's Historical Commission classified them as "significant resources" in 2003. They are also listed on the National Register of Historic Places and are included in the federal government's Historic American Buildings Survey.

However, these warehouses looked to be on the brink of total collapse in the early 2000s. Developers were capitalizing on the transition of the neighborhood into a trendy and vibrant destination and had purchased the buildings with the intent of repurposing them into apartments and condos. However, there soon was a lot of press and public outcry about how slowly renovation was progressing. When construction stalled, the rear walls and flooring of the structure collapsed. The interior was left exposed by the collapsed area, and the building seemed to be in a declining unstable condition. However, after some intervention by the city, the renovations resumed again and were eventually completed. The buildings have been rehabilitated into luxury apartments with much of their exterior architectural history intact. Unfortunately, the brick façade has been cleaned and repointed, and none of the original painted signage remains.

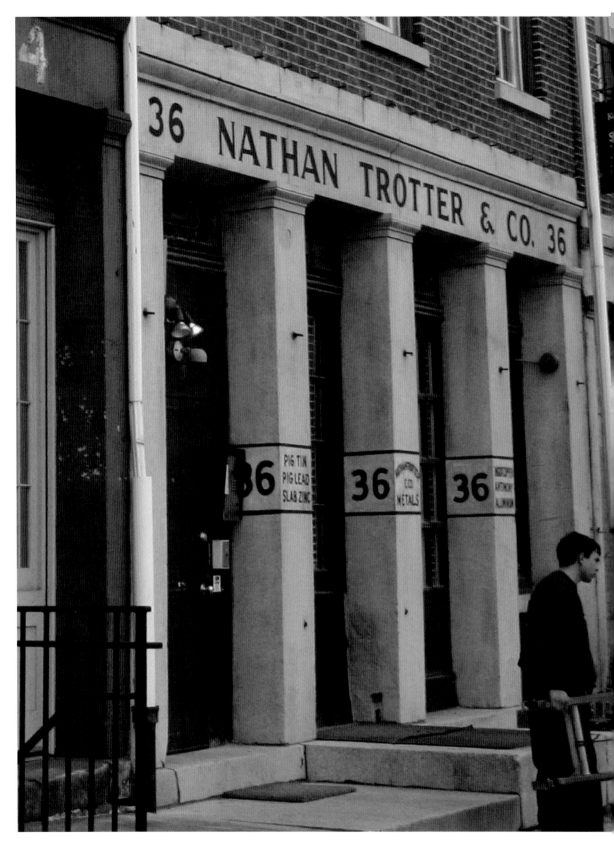

Nathan Trotter Metals

36 NORTH FRONT STREET

LEFT *Pig Tin, Pig Lead, Slab Zinc—just some of the metals and alloys available from Nathan Trotter & Co., an importer and supplier of metals to the local craftspeople in the colony. The sign has been faithfully preserved, although you can see the faint outlines of older words layered beneath this latest coat of paint. The company is still in business today, having relocated outside the city to the suburbs.*

INSET RIGHT *In this city archive photo dated 1969, we can see the Trotter storefront at the far left. Most of the signage is visible, but the "Pig Tin," "Pig Lead" and "Slab Zinc" lettering appears to have been painted over.* **Photo courtesy of PhillyHistory.org, a project of the Philadelphia Department of Records.**

Located just north from the historic Girard Estate warehouses on Front Street, the Trotter building is another surviving example of a Philadelphia from an era long ago. It too has surprisingly changed very little over the years.

Nathan Trotter was born into a middle-class Quaker family of craftsmen and entrepreneurs. His uncles and brothers were well-respected cabinetmakers, merchants and bankers throughout colonial Philadelphia. Trotter founded his namesake metal-importing company at this location in 1789, providing tin to other local colonial craftspeople who in turn converted it into pewter. The columns of the building façade feature well-maintained signage that lists the various types of strange-sounding metals and alloys that were once on offer here. This hand-painted menu displays things like "Pig Tin," "Pig Lead" and "Slab Zinc."

This particular sign—the one at street level—became important to me in the designs leading up to the construction and presentation of my senior thesis. These elements of the roughly painted "Pig Tin," "Pig Lead" and "Slab Zinc" made their way into early prototypes of the book and, by the time the thesis was designed, still held a prominent place on the prominent spread where they were featured.

More than two hundred years since its founding, Nathan Trotter & Co., Inc., is still in business and operates in the suburbs of Coatesville, Pennsylvania. The company has evolved into the largest manufacturer of tin and tin alloys in North America. The original foundry building on Front Street has since been converted into private residences but maintains the historic signage.

Furniture Industries Manufacturers Showrooms

SECOND STREET AND TROTTERS ALLEY

Located high up on the side of a building at the corner of Second Street and Trotters Alley, this is truly a ghost sign. In some light, there are clear outlines of letters (S? H? O?) but not enough to make out any sort of words. Other days, there is nothing but a runny white blotch of paint. In city archive photos from 1952 and 1972, we can see a much fresher, newer sign in this location and can discern that these newer letters read: "FURNITURE INDUSTRIES MANUFACTURERS SHOW ROOMS."

Interestingly, the more modern advertisement for Furniture Industries Manufacturers has all but disappeared, leaving behind the illegible, blotchy sign beneath it, with those large letters reversed out of white pigment. I haven't been able to find any archival imagery to match up with this older, larger sign, nor much information about the building itself. We can date the structure to about the late nineteenth century by its Victorian eclectic style of architecture.

Leas and McVitty Oak Tanners

VINE AND ORIANNA STREETS

LEFT *An old sign for Leas and McVitty Incorporated Oak Tanners, indicating this location as the Philadelphia-based home office for a number of family-owned tanneries throughout the southern states.*

This relatively modest "Leas and McVitty Incorporated Oak Tanners" advertisement appears above much more modern painted signs. The building, located on Vine and Orianna Streets, was the home office for multiple tanneries in the southeastern United States.

The family business was originally founded here in Philadelphia, but manufacturing moved south to Salem, Virginia, due to the regional availability of chestnut tree bark and the proximity to other hide finishing businesses. The extract produced from ground chestnut tree bark was used as a tanning agent to imbue leather hides with a deep, rich brown color.

The Leas and McVitty business was in operation from the mid-1800s all the way up until the early 1970s, when the Salem tannery complex was destroyed by a massive fire. I could not find much more information about the company after the fire. This Philadelphia office building has been rehabbed into condominiums, but the signage for an original inhabitant still remains.

THE BORDERS OF CENTER CITY line up fairly well with those of the original boundaries of the city of Philadelphia prior to its consolidation in 1854. Those boundaries technically include Olde City. But since we've already covered that area, we'll move on in a more westwardly direction to observe a few signs toward the city's current government and business district.

Here, we find ourselves surrounded by a decidedly more modern landscape, home of the tallest buildings in Philadelphia—monolithic glass edifices that rise hundreds of feet into the air, throwing the small forgotten alleys and streets below into perpetual shadow. My father has, in my memory, always worked in Center City. I know now that he worked at offices located in University City, but to me, all the high-rises of glass and steel appeared the same. Yet among these contemporary marvels of architecture we can still find remnants of the past that cling to the walls of the older structures.

This area, like most city centers, has long been a shopping district, as well as the home to many corporate offices and headquarters. And so here can be found an interesting mix of signage and advertising, still quietly extolling the quality of their wares to crowds of people passing by below, no longer aware of their existence.

RIGHT *A large but faint mural sign for a feature film that was screened here more than fifty years ago.*

CENTER
CITY

Texaco...Garage...Oils

BROAD AND PINE STREETS

The automobile. Early in the 1900s, the car eventually became more and more accepted as a mainstream form of transportation. But it was still slow to take hold in terms of personal ownership within the population of Philadelphia—probably to be expected in any dense urban environment. Nonetheless, the car began to make its presence known throughout the city, especially by the 1920s. With the loosely defined zoning and land-use laws of the period, gas stations, automobile dealerships and parking lots started appearing wherever space became available and business seemed viable. It was not uncommon in those early days of motoring to find gasoline stations on side streets and in the middle of residential blocks, sandwiched between single-family homes. Nowhere was this more apparent than along main commuting thoroughfares.

Take, for example, Broad Street, where just about any manner of automobile showroom and accessory retail store could be found, as well as gas stations and parking lots. Gradually, as laws for zoning caught up with these businesses, and increasing land prices in Center City demanded more income from the real estate than something such as a gas station could provide, these early establishments closed or moved on to more suitable locations. But if you look closely, clues to their presences still remain today.

Here on Broad Street, just north of Pine Street, we find a tall office building whose uninterrupted side walls are adorned with lettering that advertised goods of interest to the early motorist. Signage on the front of the building once identified this location as the Pennsylvania Garage. According to at least a few archive photos, the space served as a garage for the U.S. Marine Corps at some point as well. The south-facing side of the building, which we see here as it towers above Broad Street looking south toward oncoming traffic, features large painted words that read, "GARAGE, TEXACO [diagonally], GASOLINE, MOTOR OILS...EXAS CO."

The north-facing side of the building has a smaller painted sign at the top, one word of which reads, "GARAGE." Looking at archival photographs from the period, the lettering was at an early point covered over with brick-colored paint, and large dimensional metal lettering that was lighted with numerous incandescent bulbs was installed over it on all sides of the building. Both this tall building and the smaller building adjacent to it were garages; it is hard to tell from the archive photos if the advertisements still present today were for the tall building to which they are attached, the smaller building next door or for both.

The taller building has today become a part of the collection of area buildings that make up the campus of the Philadelphia University of the Arts. The ground-story entrance of this building has been renovated to remove all traces of the garage openings. The smaller building next door, though, is still to this day a parking garage and looks to be very much unchanged architecturally from the time of its construction in the 1920s.

As a side note, this is an excellent ghost-like sign, where in some light the painted words of the advertisement are very faded and not easily visible, and at other times in different lighting, such as in this photographed instance, the contrast makes interpreting the sign very easy.

Society Hill Furniture

1031–33 CHESTNUT STREET

Society Hill Furniture, which operated here for forty-five years, was a furniture retail mainstay on the Chestnut Street shopping district in Center City. The Schaffers, a local Philadelphia family, bought the building in 1963 and operated their well-known furniture store until closing the business and selling the building in 2008. A developer currently has plans to rehabilitate the structure but has asserted that it will preserve the historic details throughout. As of this writing, the building sits in a vacant but maintained condition.

High on the sides of the building's brick walls are beautifully composed and brightly colored painted ads for the Society Hill Furniture business. Just beneath the colorful signage on both the eastern- and western-facing walls of the building is a fairly visible advertisement for Wurlitzer. The building that Society Hill had occupied was originally constructed in 1894 and designed by Albert Dilkes. It was called the Wurlitzer Piano building, as the company had commissioned the building to serve as a showroom for its pianos.

The Rudolph Wurlitzer Company, often shortened and referred to simply as Wurlitzer, was an American company that specialized in producing fine pianos. However, it also manufactured violins, harps, organs and electric pianos, as well as woodwinds and brass instruments. But perhaps its most famous product was the jukebox, which Wurlitzer manufactured and popularized from 1933 until the present. The classic Model 1015—with its iconic shape, brightly lit colored columns and special "bubbling" accents—still remains the most recognizable jukebox of any kind and is in some form and in some markets still being manufactured today.

Over its sixty-five-year history in the United States, the company had built up a nationwide chain of more than one hundred retail stores, the most important of which were established in the major cities of Buffalo, Cincinnati, Chicago, New York and this one, located here on Chestnut Street in Philadelphia. Started in Cincinnati in 1856, the woodwind and brass instrument production ceased when the company was acquired by Baldwin Piano in 1988. The Wurlitzer name was then sold to Gibson Guitars in 2001. However, continuation and new model jukeboxes are still manufactured in Germany under the trademark name.

Stephen Girard Hotel
1031–33 CHESTNUT STREET

ABOVE *"STEPHEN GIRARD HOTEL." Signage appeared on three sides of the building at one time; now, only this rear sign remains. The building changed hotel names a few times and then was converted into a YMCA. Most recently, it houses a city charter school.*

This stately building on the far west side of Center City began its life as a hotel. Shown as the Roosevelt in 1910 city atlases, it had changed its name to the Stephen Girard Hotel by 1942. It's unclear whether or not this building was once tied to the estate of the great Philadelphia philanthropist.

At one point, large painted-letter signs reading, "STEPHEN GIRARD HOTEL" existed on either side of the building, as well as on the rear; now, only the rear sign remains visible. In 1962, the building became the home of a YMCA and, in 1999, was converted into the Freire Charter School, a college-preparatory learning experience for the underserved youth of Philadelphia.

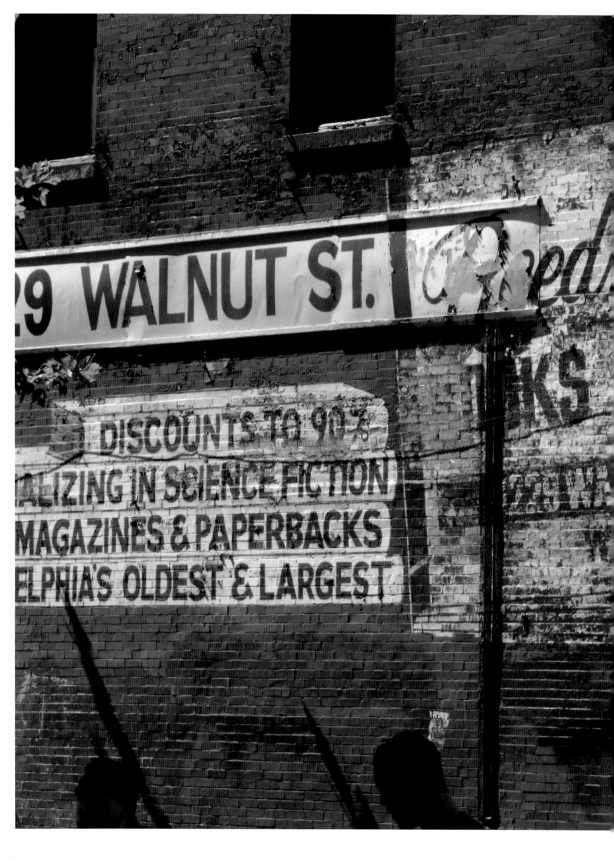

Reedmor Books

ELEVENTH AND CHESTNUT STREETS

Reedmor Books, most recently the Reedmor Magazine Company, was a Center City purveyor of discounted books and magazines. It was located a block away and around the corner from this interesting sign on Walnut Street, which made clever use of two unsightly bricked-over garage bays to advertise closer to the busy pedestrian shopping traffic on Chestnut Street. The goal was to hopefully steer a few customers off Chestnut and down to its storefront.

This sign covers the mismatched brick pattern of the garages with nicely composed lettering and illustrated sign painting. It also incorporates a prominent directional arrow, pointing you toward the store location and helping to further hide the irregularities in the wall surfaces. The store was the self-proclaimed largest and oldest of its kind in the city and, according to the sign itself, was "specializing in science fiction, back date magazines and paperbacks."

I remember this sign quite vividly from my childhood, as it was pretty interesting to me even then. The illustrated stack of books and the energetic lettering are pretty difficult to forget. I recall seeing it often enough for it to stick in my brain since my sister, who was a dancer pretty much the entire time we were kids, would shop at Baum's Dance and Theater Shop for her shoes and dancewear. Baum's is located directly next door to this sign.

The building on which this sign is painted had been left mostly vacant until 2010, when local suburban coffee chain Milkboy took over the space. It has been renovated into a café and bar on the ground level and a live music venue on the second floor. As part of the renovation, contractors reopened both of the garage bays, which did remove a small portion of the sign, but thankfully, the owners realized the inherent beauty of the lettering and have left the rest of it intact.

LEFT *Here is the painted Reedmor advertisement as it appeared prior to the bricked-over garage bays being opened back up for the current tenants. The sign has lasted quite well. Note the exchange name letters in the phone number, dating this sign to the 1960s at the latest.*

Binder, Wig and Toupee Maker
35 SOUTH THIRTEENTH STREET

LEFT *A close-up of the projecting bay window on the Binder building, with its decorative and dimensional tin lettering that reads, "Ladies' and Children's Hairdressing."*

INSET RIGHT *The signboard lettering on this building, now painted over with dark matte paint, reads, "Binder's, Wig and Toupee Maker" and "Hair Cutting and Singeing." The projecting bay window is at right, between these and the other two signboards.*

This unassuming (at first) building, dwarfed by the more modern high-rises all around it and the Wanamaker department store building directly across the street, was the home of the Binder Company—a hairdressing and shampoo parlor and makers of wigs, toupees, soaps and tonics. This type of lettered advertising—pressed metal signboards and raised dimensional lettering—is not usually considered a faded ad or ghost sign. But in this case, the sign and its history are just too interesting not to include in this collection.

Richard Binder, a Civil War veteran and recipient of the Medal of Honor, commissioned this building's construction in 1887 for the purpose of opening a hairdressing, cutting and shampooing studio. He had grown his business and become one of the most successful hairdressers in nineteenth- and early twentieth-century Philadelphia. Binder was one of only about one hundred or so professional hairdressers in the whole city—most hairdressing at that time was done privately in the home.

The signboard lettering—now covered over with a coat of flat matte paint—is quite easy to miss. But seen at the right angle, the outlines of letters begin to reveal themselves. The first signboard panel, far left at the corner of Thirteenth and Clover Streets, reads, "Binder, Wig and Toupee Maker." The next signboard panel reads, "Hair Cutting and Singeing." (Hair singeing is a centuries-old technique used in many regions of the world to give a smooth finish to a hair cut or style; singeing the ends of hair was believed to not only remove frayed, stray pieces but also to leave the ends smoothly tapered, "sealing" the cut.) The third panel reads, "Binder, Ladies' and Children's Haircutting, Dressing and Shampooing." The final signboard panel, closest to Chestnut Street, reads simply, "Cigars." The last sign seems to have been unrelated to the Binder business.

In the middle of the beautifully arched series of windows on the second story is a projecting bay window featuring a full panel with beautiful dimensional tin lettering, which reads "Ladies' and Children's Hairdressing." It's amazing how the monotone paint covering the lettering and the exterior lighting that places emphasis on the renovated street-level deli below have worked so effectively that these signs have now become rather easy to overlook. This is one of those signs that, when you finally do focus on it and see the lettering, you can't believe you hadn't seen it before. It's rather amazing.

Midtown Theater
1412 CHESTNUT STREET, REAR

The Karlton Theater, an Italianate-style, marble-decorated second-run movie theater, opened here on Chestnut Street between Broad and Fifteenth Streets in October 1921. After a few decades of success, local Philadelphia theater operator William Goldman acquired the Karlton in 1943 and changed its format into a first-run movie theater. However, the Karlton closed on October 16, 1950, due to rising competition from other newer, more up-to-date nearby theaters. The idea of a thirty-year-old theater wasn't popular with the public, who were looking for something more modern. Drastic exterior renovations were designed and carried out by architect David Supowitz, meant to revive new life and modernize the theater inside and out. Decidedly mid-century in aesthetic, green plastic covered most of the old classically styled façade, and huge sculpted metal

letters spelling out the theater's new name, Midtown, were mounted so that they appeared to float over the plastic. The Midtown Theater opened on December 23, 1950.

Two decades later, in the early 1970s, William Goldman sold his theaters to another local operator. This operator, Budco, "twinned" the theater's original single auditorium by building a wall right down the middle. The new twin Midtown Theater reopened on June 13, 1980, with *The Shining* showing on both screens. Budco eventually sold its theaters to the American Multi-Cinema chain, known these days by its acronym AMC, which operated the Midtown until lagging attendance forced its closure in 1995.

It's a shame too—I was always interested in the architecture of this

structure but never attended a movie here. There were closer theaters to my house in South Philadelphia. The emptying of people from Center City after the workday and on the weekends during the '80s and '90s was incredible. It was as if the city's sidewalks rolled up. Not until recently has that trend reversed and has Center City become a destination again.

In another twist of fate, as part of that reclamation of Center City as a destination for more than just the nine-to-five workday, the theater was purchased and renovated into a live theater in 1999. The theater was renamed the Prince Music Theater in honor of Broadway producer and director Harold "Hal" Prince. Hal has been involved with many of the best-known musical productions of the past fifty years. Hal attended the University of Pennsylvania, was active in the theater scene here and has thus become an honorary Philadelphian. The exterior of the Prince Music Theater still resembles the 1950s Midtown Theater exterior, although the undulating green plastic has been replaced with aluminum.

If you travel west down Sansom Street, along a quiet stretch between Broad and Fifteenth Streets, about halfway down the block you'll arrive at the brick back wall of the theater. There, a huge faux billboard still remains, still featuring the last movie advertisement painted there. The Midtown hosted Philadelphia stops for road shows of anticipated epic movies. One such epic to stop at the theater was director Michael Anderson's film adaptation of the Jules Verne novel *Around the World in Eighty Days*, shown at the theater in 1956. After this show moved on, it seems the billboard, which did not (and to this day still does not) receive much attention from either vehicular or foot traffic, was abandoned. It would appear that at some point the ad had been whitewashed, but over the years the elements have slowly helped reveal this advertisement for a coming attraction from over fifty years ago.

The Pitcairn Building
TWELFTH AND ARCH STREETS

LEFT *A view of the present-day sign on the eastern-facing wall of the Pitcairn Building. Here was can see a well-weathered mixture of Pittsburgh Plate Glass Company and H. Daroff and Sons advertisements on the wall facing east toward the traffic on Arch Street.*

The Pitcairn Building is an elegant and understated eight-story commercial building located at the corner of Twelfth and Arch Streets. The building was designed by the famous Philadelphia architects G.W. and W.D. Hewitt, who also designed other local landmarks such as the Bourse and the Bellevue-Stratford Hotel. A quoin on the building marks the year when construction was completed as 1901.

The building was named for John Pitcairn, president and co-founder of the Pittsburgh Plate Glass Company, which is still in business today and is better known by the acronym PPG. The company used this building as offices and for warehousing space until 1923, when PPG moved out and the property was acquired by the H. Daroff and Sons Company.

By the 1880s, the clothing industry was becoming highly mechanized, and by the early twentieth century, production was able to move from large spaces outside the city into more compact and efficient loft buildings in Center City, similar to those of the Pitcairn Building. Prior to its acquisition by Daroff and Sons, PPG had leased portions of the building to other clothing manufacturers. Interestingly, at some point during this time, the two upper floors of the building had been used as a bowling alley and a skating rink.

The Daroff Company was one of the major clothing manufacturers located in Philadelphia in the early 1900s. By the 1920s, the company was contributing a considerable portion of suits to the total 3.6 million men's suits produced annually by all of the clothing manufacturers in the city. The Daroff Company grew its business dramatically while located in the Pitcairn Building and by the 1940s had become a nationally recognized company. At this point, it needed to expand, and so it moved to a larger location at Twenty-third and Walnut Streets in 1945 after it

acquired the Philadelphia-based Botany 500 brand and fabric mill. Through an unprecedented marketing strategy, Daroff brought its brands to national attention by outfitting and promoting celebrities and television game show hosts with its brand of suits.

The Pitcairn Building has been recently rehabilitated into loft condominiums called "1027 Arch Street Lofts." Thankfully, the advertisements on the east wall have been left intact, although they have weathered badly. One can just about make out a faint "Daroff" in large lettering along the top of the sign, a remnant of the later clothing business, and a fairly legible "PAINT" right across the middle of the sign, a remnant of the days when Pittsburg Plate Glass occupied the site and advertised here.

The Cunningham Building

1312–1314 CHESTNUT STREET

LEFT *The letters of "Cunningham Pianos" can be seen running vertically along the walls of this building on Chestnut Street, painted directly over the decorative brick and stonework.*

The Cunningham Building is a tall, thin and impressive structure made of pale yellow brick and devoid of much ornamentation. The structure is as wide as two plots but runs street to street from Chestnut Street at front to the small alley of Drury Street behind. It appears that at one time, letters were painted on the masonry on the upper floors of the building and then at a later time either covered with metal signage or squares of black paint. The brick along the east and west walls is covered with odd patches of signage and advertising. Whatever the reasoning or situation, we can still make out the letters of "Cunningham Pianos" running vertically along the walls looking east and west on Chestnut Street, as well as stone lettering in a limestone signboard with the words "Cunningham Building" in a belt around the upper stories.

Cunningham Piano Company was started in 1891 by Patrick J. Cunningham, who immigrated to Philadelphia from Ireland. The company he started manufactured its own make of acoustic upright and fine grand pianos. Through an unwavering commitment to quality and with keen business acumen on behalf of the management, the Cunningham Piano Company quickly became one of the nation's most respected makers of pianos. While the factory building that manufactured the pianos was located in West Philadelphia, this building on Chestnut Street was constructed in 1920, at the height of the brand's popularity, and served as the official Cunningham Piano offices and showrooms.

However, the Great Depression and the years following took a huge toll on business throughout the area, as well as the nation as a whole. Just before the outbreak of World War II, Cunningham Piano Company sadly ceased the production of pianos. The company did remain open, and is still in business today, but it has moved from this location to a much smaller facility in Germantown, Pennsylvania, just outside the city. The company now focuses on the restoration of fine pianos of all makes and styles.

The Chestnut Street building has seen use as an office space in the decades since Cunningham packed up and moved out of its headquarters. The PMC Group, a chemical and plastics manufacturer, was one of the last tenants, but the building has sat vacant for some time since that company moved to New Jersey. In 2007, the high-rise building and the small storefront immediately adjacent to it were purchased by the Church of Scientology. Having outgrown its current location on Race Street, the church plans to renovate the properties into a center that will include a chapel, offices, an academy and displays about the church's community programs. As of this writing, the building still sits unused.

THE CALLOWHILL AREA of Philadelphia, the former home of many large-scale manufacturing and other industrial enterprises, was originally named after Hannah Callowhill Penn, William Penn's second wife. A rich architectural history has been left behind by the period of manufacturing in this area: grand factories, expansive warehouses, remnants of long-forgotten trades and a maze of arched stone railroad viaducts and trestled overpasses that snake in, around and through these buildings.

In the period of deindustrialization in major American cities throughout the 1950s, this neighborhood was all but emptied of its population, as many companies relocated to the suburbs or shuttered, and the local residential workforce followed suit along with them. It is still an eerily quiet and secluded pocket of the city, despite its relatively centralized location. But now, as real estate ventures have begun looking at interesting investments in untapped areas, developers have begun converting some of these large remaining buildings into loft-style housing. This has earned the neighborhood the new title of "Loft District," and the revitalization efforts are luring people back into becoming residents here once more.

Even with population numbers rising again, the area remains a relatively sparsely populated section of the city. But that lack of population has meant that the neighborhood has not changed too dramatically, and there are still interesting faded advertisements to be discovered here.

RIGHT *A large mural made up of many colorful layers of overlapping signs on the Esslinger Brewery.*

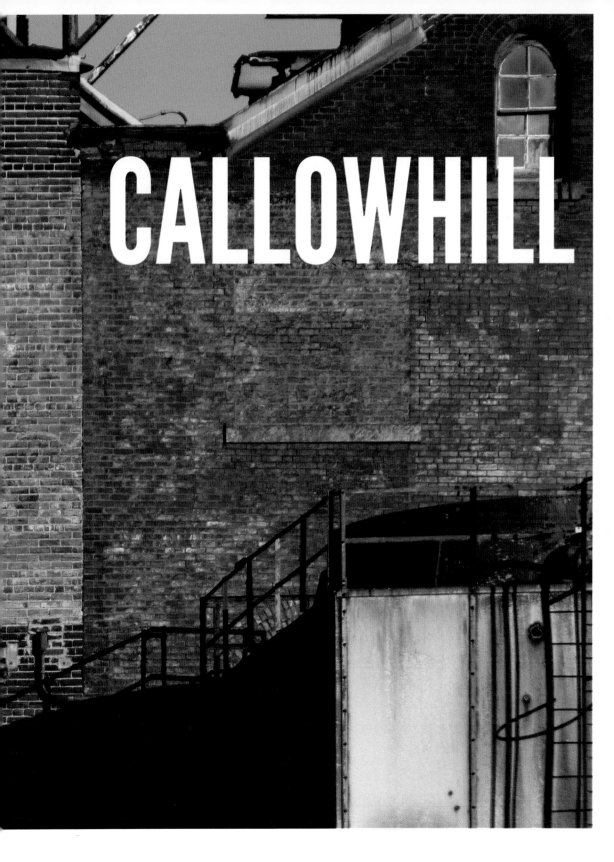

F. WEBER
MANUFACTURER
ARTISTS COLORS
Supplies for Architects, Drau...

STONE...

PPLY INC.
MP
LAMP
STAL LAMP

F. Weber and Company

BUTTONWOOD BETWEEN ELEVENTH AND TWELFTH STREETS

Anyone who has ever dabbled in oil painting or pastel drawing or has gone into any art supply or craft store has at some point come across a Weber product of some sort. Established in 1853 as an art supplies sales agency, the company grew through strategic partnerships and corporate acquisitions to eventually become F. Weber and Company in 1887. This company is the oldest and one of the largest manufacturers of art supplies in the United States. It has, over the years, offered a wide range of imported and self-manufactured products such as artists' supplies, painting and drawing supplies, mathematical instruments, materials for gilders, sign and coach-painters, china decorators, engineers, lithographers, etchers and engravers, materials for pyrography and wax and paper flowers.

The disruption of commerce during World War I caused artists in America to rethink their dependency on the supply of European-made materials. They instead began to rely more on American-made art supplies, which created both a need and an opportunity for Weber to expand its own manufacturing capabilities. By the early 1920s, in addition to its manufacturing and distribution facilities located at this building, F. Weber and Company also had three separate retail stores, one located in Center City Philadelphia, one in Baltimore and the last in St. Louis.

A number of patents for innovative products have been awarded to the company. One of the most notable was for Weber's Original Permalba White paint, which was first formulated in 1921. With this product, Weber was the first to develop and market a non-toxic, opaque, white oil paint to replace the toxic, lead-based whites that artists had been using for hundreds of years prior.

This building is listed as the Main Office and Factory in period advertisements placed by the firm. It is also listed as a research lab, with Weber himself credited as the technical director, with two fellow chemists on staff. The company is still in business, having been acquired by Martin, another art supply company, and has since been relocated to Northeast Philadelphia. This building, located on Buttonwood Street between Eleventh and Twelfth Streets, has been converted into loft apartments.

The large lettered sign along the side of the building reads, "F. Weber Co., Manufacturers of Artists Colors (&) Materials, Supplies for Architects, Dra(ughts)men & Engineers. Blueprint Papers. Store 1125 Ch(est)nut." The symbol on the elevator machine room at the top appears to be the Weber sphinx logo with the words "TRADE MARK" below. I had often seen this sign when washing my car at the Wash and Lube on Spring Garden Street. But because of the strange angle of view and the relatively small size of the building, I could never quite pinpoint the sign's exact location. One day, after a car wash, I drove over and circled each block until I figured out where it was.

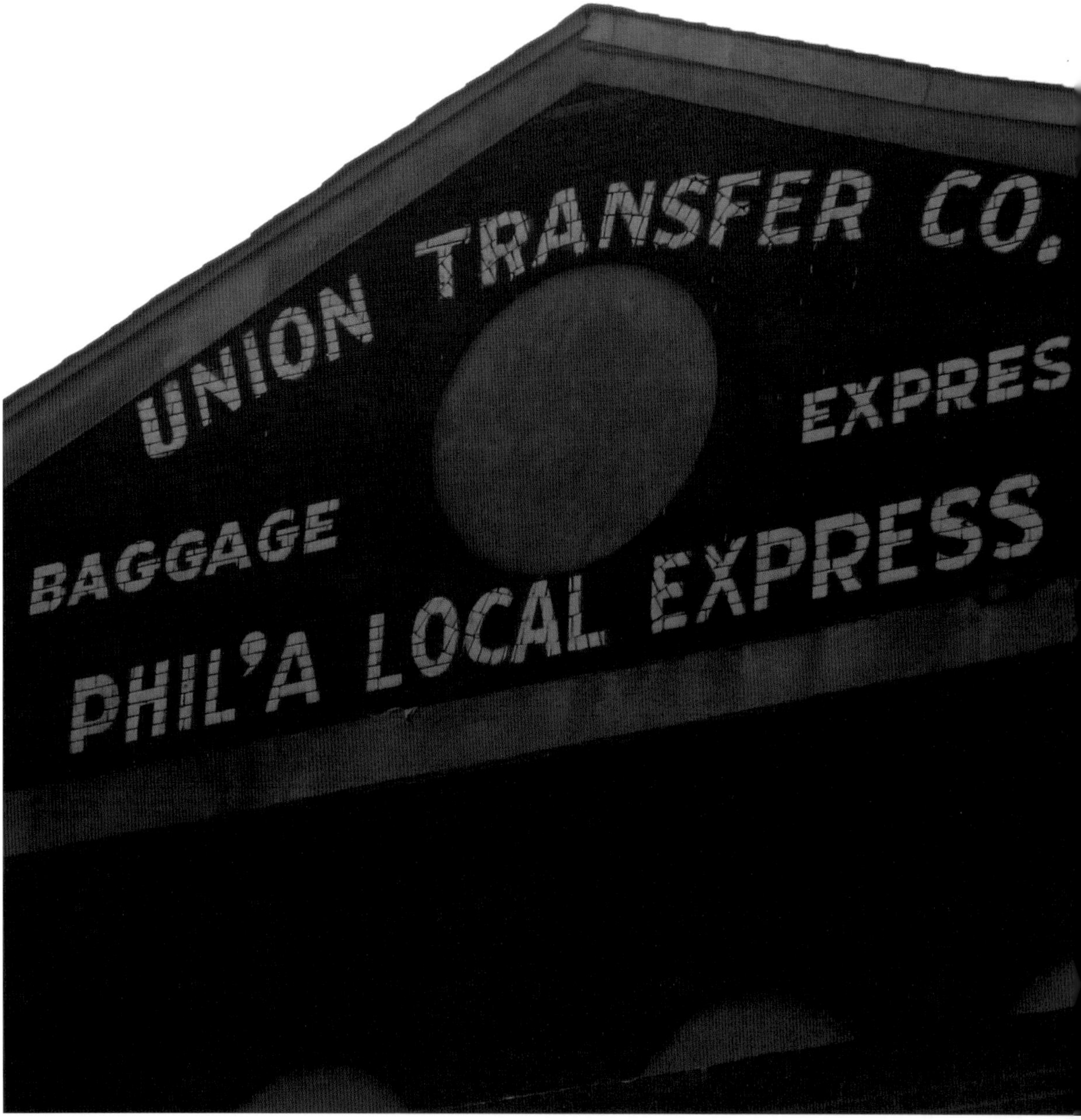
UNION TRANSFER CO.
BAGGAGE
EXPRES
PHIL'A LOCAL EXPRESS

Union Transfer Company

SPRING GARDEN AND TENTH STREETS

The Union Transfer Company was an express baggage transportation firm that first incorporated in 1867 in Philadelphia. Records show the company was in business continuously through at least 1918 and most likely survived longer than that. Union Transfer had local branch offices in Atlantic City, Cape May and Camden, New Jersey, and eventually spread to cities farther south such as Baltimore, Maryland, and Washington, D.C. The 1100 Chestnut Street Branch Office address first appears in Philadelphia city directory listings in the mid-1880s. There are numerous styles of archive trade cards that depict illustrations of a horse-drawn express wagon, typical of the early pre-motorized fleet the company employed. The wooden-slatted sides of the carriages had the lettering "Union Transfer Company, Baggage Express" painted on them.

In 1886, the Pennsylvania Railroad Company initiated a new "special delivery system" for baggage, which employed the New York Transfer Company in New York and the Union Transfer Company in Philadelphia, Baltimore and Washington as part of the system. Passengers could ship baggage in advance from any address in one city to any address in any one of the other member cities, freeing up those passengers from the problems of dealing with handling heavy and numerous baggage items when traveling.

This half-block-long warehouse building, located on Spring Garden between Tenth and Eleventh Streets, is a beautiful architectural mix of brick and red stone details. The building was utilitarian in nature, serving as a warehouse and staging area for baggage and freight. There is very little signage present on the building, only some lettering at either end of the long warehouse that reads, "Union Transfer Co., Baggage Express, Phil'a Local Express."

The space itself has served many purposes since the baggage handling days: freight warehouse, market, daycare center, automotive repair shop and Spaghetti Warehouse chain restaurant. Our family had visited the restaurant a few times when it first opened. The cavernous interior was a sight to behold. The restaurant housed a few trolley cars inside, apparently something the chain did in many of its locations. You could sit inside the trolleys for dinner, which of course I always insisted upon.

A recent visit to the site confirms that the sign has recently been retouched, as the space has been renovated and repurposed yet again. This time it has been converted into a live music venue, which aptly borrows the name "Union Transfer."

George Esslinger's Brewery

TENTH STREET, RIDGE AVENUE AND CALLOWHILL STREET

At the intersection of Tenth Street, Ridge Avenue and Callowhill Street Esslinger's Brewery was in business from 1873 to 1920 and then again from 1933 until its eventual close in 1964. It was one of several large regional breweries that operated in Philadelphia's independent beer-producing height during the 1940s and 1950s. It was also one of only a handful of breweries that reopened after the forced shuttering during Prohibition. There are a number of buildings in this complex, built in different eras, some of which have been demolished. The newest of the buildings is Plant No. 1 and is marked as such with engraved stones above the doors at street level.

To compete successfully post-Prohibition, the Esslinger brand employed a waiter mascot in its advertising and marketing efforts. He was called the "Little Man," and he became the namesake of its bestselling Little Man Ale. The Esslinger identity was lettered in a calligraphic script face and, for many years, was reproduced on the front of its iconic bright yellow and red cans. Some of these colors are still visible in the remnants of advertising on the walls of the plant itself

High on the side of the brewery, we find a series of colorful overlapping panels with ads of varying age. These signs are not easily visible when standing in front of the brewery at the intersection of Tenth Street and Ridge. However, those signs do not seem to be meant for the pedestrian on the street. Instead, the ads were placed at this

height to be easily visible from trains traveling along the neighboring elevated Reading Railroad viaduct, which passes by less than a block away.

An older, larger sign with the first few letters of the curvaceous "Esslinger" script peeking through is covered by newer, yellow-background sign. Another sign appears far beneath, located low on one of the older parts of the jigsaw-like complex. The only remaining legible section reads, "...& SON." This could be a remnant of signage for the G. Dallett & Son Co., a candle and soap works that occupied this corner space until moving farther up Ridge Avenue in 1880. This particular part of the sign is located

on what looks to be the oldest of the adjoined brick buildings that make up the complex; brickwork and window styles indicate that the structure might be a surviving part of the earlier soap works. Archival illustration depicts both George Esslinger's Brewery & Lager Beer Garden and Dallett's Soap & Candle Manufactury [sic] as one-time neighbors on this corner in 1884.

After the Esslinger brewery closed for good, the plant was occupied by National Chemical Laboratories Incorporated, a cleaning and maintenance chemical supplies company. With a combined inventory of over three million gallons of raw material and finished products, it is the largest company of its kind

in the United States. The company still operates from this complex of buildings to this day. The brick along the east and west walls is covered with odd patches of signage and advertising.

Edwin J. Cummings Family and Steam Coal House

CALLOWHILL STREET AT THE NOBLE STREET OVERPASS

This small shed structure is all that is left from the days when coal yards dominated the areas alongside the Reading Railroad viaduct, particularly along this stretch of Callowhill Street. Coal was essential to both the economic success of the Philadelphia and Reading Railroad (P&R) and to the industry that operated close to the center of the city. The P&R was specifically built to bring anthracite from the coal regions of Pennsylvania down into Philadelphia for use in powering local industrial plants, as well as for the heating of residential homes

This particular shed was once a part of the Edwin J. Cummings Family & Steam Coal Yard. This singular structure is all that remains of the complex of buildings; the rest of the yard was razed and turned into a parking lot decades ago. The other area coal yards that had once occupied

the real estate alongside the train tracks have long since disappeared as well. Most of the signs on the façade of this small structure are illegible, having long since weathered away, but on the bottom right wall you can still make out a bit of lettering that reads "CUMMINGS COAL."

Recently, the small building was opened up to the public for a tour, and a store of tools and a collection of coal and railroad memorabilia were found inside. Some of these items dated back to the Cummings Coal–era of operation. The building is in remarkably good shape. The current owners of the building, a family that has owned the land for generations, hopes to one day restore the structure for future conversion into a restaurant, commercial or retail space and also hopes to use these nostalgic items stored within as part of the renovation.

Adam Steinmetz
Steam Marble Works

RIDGE AVENUE AND HAMILTON STREET

This sign is pretty easy to miss and very difficult to see, since it's mostly obscured from view by a building that did not exist here until recently. The only way I was able to find its exact location was by cross-referencing historical atlases with the bird's-eye-view satellite imagery from various online mapping sites.

The Adam Steinmetz Steam Marble Works manufactured and sold marble mantels, furniture tops, statuary, tiling, gravestones and other sepulchral monuments from an open-air yard just off Ridge Avenue. The inclusion of "steam" in the company name indicates that steam machinery was used in the manufacturing process. I was able to decipher much of the wording on the sign by matching it up to an archived trade card from the business itself. The yard used to be located in an L-shaped plot of land that at one time had access to both Ridge Avenue and Hamilton Street at either end. The negative space that the yard once occupied has now been filled in completely by buildings. However, the advertisements that used to line the inward-facing walls of the yard are still visible just above the roofline of the new one-story building that faces Ridge Avenue.

A complex sign situated at what would have been one of the entrances to the yard reads, "A. Steinmetz Marble Works, MARBLE MANTLES...STAND and FURNITURE TOPS, MONUMENTS." A large signband that runs what appears to be the length of the yard reads, "...STONES" in tall lettering, presumably forming the word "TOMBSTONES" or "GRAVESTONES." I cannot see far enough back into the space to determine for sure what the first few letters of that sign might be.

Haverford Bicycle Company
TENTH AND BUTTONWOOD STREETS

City records indicate that Max Sladkin, the owner of the Haverford Bicycle Company, purchased this large property at Tenth and Buttonwood to manufacture his line of bicycles and bicycle parts around 1919. Sladkin was moving his existing business here from a smaller shop that was located farther south on Market Street.

The brazen corporate slogan "The Bicycle with the National Reputation" is painted almost the entire length in huge letters near the top on both sides of the building. Running vertically along the northern edges of the building are the faded words "BLACK BEAUTY," which corresponds to a line of bicycle models that Haverford Bicycle Company, or HBC, offered. It is not certain, but perhaps the smaller diagonal signage between windows—"NORFOLK," "NEWARK," "BRA...ES"—could be cities where other

showrooms were located, in keeping with the "national reputation" slogan. It's difficult to tell, as the signs on this building have not held up very well.

There are numerous overlapping signs all over the building, in this case many of them painted directly over the same areas as earlier signs in order to hide the older ones. As these signs weather away and expose their layers, the individual signs become harder and harder to interpret. There are signs for "Leather Goods" and "Bags," along with floor directories and other names of the various companies that have since occupied the building. The signs are located high on the eastern-facing wall of the building and butted up against each wall edge, in order to be seen above and around the police and fire stations that once stood next-door.

All across the building, there are also numerous references to "Paper Goods," which is typical of many factories in the area and many factories in the city in general. Philadelphia in the late 1800s had the distinction of becoming the largest producer of paper boxes in the United States. At its height, Philadelphia's paper box industry employed up to 1,900 men and women. It would seem that some business in this building at one time played a contributing role in that industry.

ALCO Clothes,
Frank C. Maurone Co., Inc.

ELEVENTH AND WOOD STREETS

LEFT *"ALCO Clothes," the name shortened from Arnold Louchheim & Company, was a men's apparel manufacturer and wholesaler that occupied this building from its construction. An older sign is very faintly visible beneath. The sign faces away from Center City toward the elevated railroad tracks nearby.*

A men's apparel manufacturer and wholesaler, the Arnold Louchheim & Company (which through common use had been shortened to ALCO), is listed as doing business in this building as far back as 1906. The sign is located high up on the corner of Eleventh and Carlton Streets, which at first appears odd since it faces north, away from the center of the city and the direction of traffic along Eleventh Street, which the building fronts. But the sign was placed here so it could be seen from the trains traveling along the elevated tracks of the Reading Railroad viaduct, which crosses Eleventh in clear view of the building just a block north.

The "ALCO Clothes" sign, with its large yet straightforward letters, is hiding an older sign that is slowly reappearing from beneath. It is difficult to tell what that sign could have been advertising—it appears to have some sort of illustration. The building is shown in atlases as belonging to Arnold Louchheim & Company in 1910, but in earlier atlases dated 1895, there are row homes in place of this six-story building, which means the structure had not yet been built.

On the opposite side of the very same building, at the corner of Eleventh and Wood Streets, a more colorful and modern ad can be found. A painted advertisement for "Frank C. Maurone Co. Inc., Wholesale Distributors, Bazaar & Carnival Supplies, 25 years," rises vertically along the corner edge of the building, complete with an illustration of a cheerful teddy bear holding balloons. Nearby, there is directional signage reading, "Shipping Receiving," with an arrow pointing down Wood Street. These signs are currently covered by temporary printed fabric banner signage for the art gallery that now occupies a few floors of the space. Unfortunately, the Maurone Company is no longer in operation; the company was in business from 1974 until 2001.

John Evans' Sons, Inc.

THIRTEENTH AND NECTARINE STREETS

LEFT *This was the original home of John Evans' Sons, Inc, the country's oldest operating spring-making business. Aside from the fading of black pigment, the signage on this building appears to be mostly unaltered from that of the late 1800s.*

John Evans, a blacksmith by trade, originally produced flat suspension springs for horse-drawn buggies and carriages, as well as the machinery and apparatus to produce these products. His business began in New Haven, Connecticut, in 1850. Yielding to the continued insistence by Philadelphia Spring Works, one of his largest customers, Evans moved his operation from New Haven to Philadelphia. The business arrived at this building, located at the corner of Thirteenth and Nectarine Streets, and it would reside here from 1870 until 1967. Still in business today, the company is operating just outside the city in the suburb of Lansdale, Pennsylvania. It is America's oldest spring-making company.

The building is covered in nicely lettered signage, which is still quite visible, probably due to its upkeep until the late '60s. There have been a few small adjustments to the lists of products painted between the windows since the company took up residence, but that aside, the signage appears to be largely unaltered from that of the late 1800s. "Springs, Coil, Flat, Wire Forms, Metal Stampings" fill the left panel, and the right panel reads, "Springs Tested—Heat Treated." Under the right sign, we can make out the words "Mfrs" and "Generic." On either side of the product-listing panels are interesting logos made up of painted illustrations of springs. The structure and signage are still holding up pretty well, despite the building being vacant for a number of years.

This grouping of signs in particular comes from a very interesting part of Philadelphia. It seems that a lot in these empty streets has not changed for decades. There are wider, faster, much better-lit streets to get you where you are going, and the subway runs just a few more blocks over. There's not a lot happening here and not many reasons to travel through. As such, the place is eerily quiet, and the buildings seem exactly as sullen, dark and soot-covered as they do in their black-and-white archival photographs.

"THE LIBERTIES" was a term used by William Penn, founder of the Commonwealth of Pennsylvania and planner of the colony city of Philadelphia, to describe the tracts of land lying just to the north and west of the original boundaries of his colony. It contained what was called "the liberty land" or "free lots," and they were named as such because the proprietors gave any purchaser of land within the colony, according to the amount of their purchase, a portion of these tracts of land outside the colony for free. This land policy was common practice throughout Britain and its other colonies in the New World and around the globe. Penn's original idea was to lay out a "great town" of ten thousand acres using this practice, giving lots within the city limits to early purchasers. However, surveyors found it difficult to fit these plots within the natural layout of the colony's terrain. When Penn himself arrived in the colony in 1682 and surveyed the land, he decided instead to divide the city into two parts: one that would be called the city and the other, the Liberties.

The location of these plots just outside the city limits proved an ideal setting for a great variety of manufacturing industries. Mills, breweries, leather tanneries, paints and chemical works, tool making factories, stove works and iron foundries could perform their loud, dirty and dangerous work in a space well outside the tight confines and close residential setting of the city itself. Residential areas sprung up around the factories to support the workforce that toiled in the factories. Eventually, the city's growth crept farther and farther northward and surrounded these once isolated areas. The resulting mix of historical eras of architecture is evident throughout the present-day neighborhood, as residential row homes butt up against warehouses and factories. This quirkiness and interesting shift in scale and time period is what helps make the Northern Liberties an interesting place to live and work today.

Over the past few years, the area has enjoyed a revival of sorts, as an influx of students, artists and young professionals have repopulated the neighborhood. The proximity to both Old City and Center City, as well as easy access to major public transportation and highways, has made this area one of the city's more desirable development districts, for both commercial and residential real estate, and as such, large-scale improvement and revitalization projects have been undertaken.

Unfortunately, this rapid revitalization has been stripping the neighborhood of some of its charm, as more and more original buildings are demolished to make way for development projects. With their demolition goes their history in advertising as signage.

I lived in the Northern Liberties for many years and saw much of the early stages of this transformation taking place. I remember the amazing mass of the Schmidt's Brewery, something so large it appeared to be hewn from one solid block stone. Even though it was vacant, it was such a fixture of the neighborhood that it was simply unfathomable that it could no longer be there. Many of the signs I had meant to capture and record for this book had met the wrecking ball as well, and sadly, they were gone before I could properly photograph and document them. But a few do remain for now, and the following are a few of the more interesting ones.

RIGHT *Detail of the Blue Ribbon Malt Extract sign, near Front Street.*

THE NORTHERN LIBERTIES

ACE Rental Service

THIRD STREET AND FAIRMOUNT AVENUE

This building at the corner of Third Street and Fairmount Avenue had been vacant for many years. I remember even in my earliest days visiting the neighborhood, long before living just up the street, seeing this brightly colored list of items on a building that was otherwise devoid of any other signage (with the exception of a For Sale sign). Slowly but surely, graffiti cover-up efforts—big swathes of matte red brick paint—crept higher and higher around the beltline of the first story of the building until only the very top of this sign remained visible. All that can be read at the time this photo was taken is "ACE Rental Service, Bars, Fixtures." Older images of the building I've seen on the Internet archives show more of the lettering of the items exposed, listing such industry necessities as "chinaware, glassware, silver trays, folding chairs, coffee urns and coat racks."

A little digging though the city archives uncovered this photo of the business from a warm day in 1955; note the open door of the store and the open windows of the car. Here, we can see the full business name is "Ace Bar Supply, Bar Restaurant & Janitor Supply." The shiny enameled metal storefront façade (Or is it polished stone? It's difficult to tell.) has been hand painted with lettering on both sides. Neon signs and neon borders frame the nicely organized window displays. We see an earlier version of the painted sign at left, with dimensional edge trim applied. The sign touts that Ace is "featuring a complete line of bar, restaurant, janitor and hotel supplies" and proceeds to list them: "bar stools, bar fixtures, drainboards, bar fittings, dart boards, hose & coil, glass ware, beer dispensers, china ware, rods taps & spigots, silver ware, beer compressors,

paper products, mops & brooms, juices flavors, disinfectants, cherries, soap powders, floor wax, sweeping compounds." Sounds like they have everything covered!

The façade was removed decades ago, leaving behind only this painted sign as a reminder of the business that once occupied the site. Even this sign is now completely gone, as the building has been renovated and its brick face cleaned and repainted. The old storefront now serves as the home of the Northern Liberties Neighbors Association Community Center.

Philadelphia Belting Company

SIXTH AND SPRING GARDEN STREETS

LEFT *A close-up of the Philadelphia Belting Company lettering. Note how the "tails" of each stacked word, which contain knocked-out secondary words, mimic the leather belts that the company manufactured.*

I've found surprisingly little information about this company. City atlases show only industrial use at the site in 1910 and don't label the business. I was able to learn that the company manufactured belting for use with engines (as opposed to those used in keeping up one's pants), and its "Superbelt" product was promoted as delivering "the full horsepower." I was able to track down records for a copyright of a catalogue for the firm's "Superbelt" product from December 1917. It is most likely that the horsepower was not referring to engines used for transportation purposes, as this product was being advertised during the very early days of motoring; rather it is most likely advertising the type of belts used in overhead belt-driven tools and equipment, still in common use in factories of the time.

Lettering on the westerly facing wall of this structure, looking down Spring Garden at Sixth Street, is featured in a nicely designed composition. An italicized "Philadelphia Belting Company" is stacked in three parts, each word having an underlying belt-like "tail." Within each of these tails, the secondary messaging is knocked out, reading, "MANUFACTURERS LEATHER BELTING." The background field is not a uniform square, which leads us to believe that it was shaped to clear the roofline of a building next door, which no longer stands. The sign is repeated in smaller scale on the sides of the bricked-in water tower pedestal at the rooftop, although it is difficult to see these now, as cellular phone repeaters and cabling have been mounted directly to the brick on top of them.

The building has been in sporadic use as a nightclub for many years—I admit that I've been there on more than a few occasions—and sadly, I think it still serves that purpose. Perhaps someday it will be renovated and given a new lease on life, with sympathy to the exterior signage that makes it so unique.

Premium Blue Ribbon Malt Extract

WILDEY AND FRONT STREETS

LEFT *A privilege sign for "Premium Blue Ribbon Malt Extract." This advertisement is for a product with an interesting history that can be traced back to the Prohibition era. Its use in producing beer at home circumvented the law but made it popular. The sign is located half a block away from the former location of the massive Schmidt's Brewery; one wonders if this was intentional.*

Blue Ribbon Malt Extract has a very interesting history whose origins can be traced directly back to beer. For example, the name "Blue Ribbon" comes from the blue ribbons that were tied around the Pabst Blue Ribbon beer bottlenecks, a practice that ran from 1882 until 1916. But that's not the only connection.

During the Prohibition years of the 1920s, the Pabst Brewing Company, as well as most other breweries, halted its production of alcohol and shuttered its brewing facilities. While it was closed for what seemed at the time might be indefinitely, Pabst sought a way to somehow put its machinery to use and make some sort of profit. The Perlstein brothers bought a controlling interest in the Pabst Brewing plants and changed the name of the company to Premier Malt Products, Inc. This new company used the existing equipment in the brewing plant to produce canned malts, both with and without hops, under the trade name of Blue Ribbon Malt.

Blue Ribbon Malt products were packaged and marketed as malts for homemakers to use in the baking of cakes and cookies. These goods were available at grocery stores all across America. As innocent as that may seem, and contrary to what the marketing of these products portrayed, the most practiced use for Blue Ribbon Malt products was in the brewing of beer at home, as beer was no longer legally for sale in the United States during the Prohibition years.

In 1933, when the era of Prohibition came to an end, the Pabst family reacquired its breweries and resumed the production of beer. However, having discovered the growing demand for the "Blue Ribbon" products, as well as the popularity of malt in commercial baking and cereal manufacturing, the Pabst family decided to continue the manufacturing of these products within its breweries. In 1981, the malt business was purchased from Pabst by private investors. To this day, the Premier Malt Products company manufactures, sells and distributes the same malt extracts that were sold during Prohibition.

Located at the desolate corner of Wildey and Front Street, this ad for Blue Ribbon Malt Extract is painted on a building that currently serves as offices for General Marine Refrigeration Corporation, established in 1947. It is not apparent what the relationship of the previous building's business was to the subject matter of the ad at the time of its installation—perhaps there was a store selling groceries here at one point, or perhaps it was the proximity to the once sprawling Schmidt's Brewery at the opposite end of the block. City atlases are no help in identifying what was here around the time of Prohibition. There are remnants of an older sign here as well, but due to weathering, it is not clear what appears beneath. Unfortunately, in an effort to clean, or rather mask, the building of graffiti, the lower half of the sign has been painted over in a few mismatched layers of brick-red paint.

Piedmont Cigarettes

POPLAR STREET AND ST. JOHN NEUMANN WAY

High up at the very edge of a sharply triangular building sits this lonely, weathered advertisement. It is very difficult to decipher, given its condition and what is visible. We can distinguish some sort of script lettering, starting with "P" and ending with "-mont." There is also a price callout of "5¢." With these clues, and a little cross-examination, we can determine that the script, colors and general overall layout are consistent with other Piedmont Cigarette wall ads.

Piedmont was one of the most popular cigarette brands around the year 1910; this helps date this sign to that era. Undoubtedly, the cigarette brand's popularity was bolstered by the practice of inserting baseball cards in the retail cigarette packs. In fact, some of the rarest, most collectible and highly sought-after baseball cards in the collector's market come from cigarette manufacturers like Piedmont.

Given the advertisements' subject matter and location, it is most likely a privilege sign, as the narrow first floor of this building, formed by the intersection of the skinny Poplar Street and impossibly tiny Saint John Neumann Way, was a store, bar or restaurant at that time, as shown in city atlases of the era.

LEFT *A close-up of the Piedmont Cigarettes privilege sign, found high on the edge of a triangular-shaped building formed by the intersection of two narrow streets in the Northern Liberties. Note the logotype script and the faint illustration of the cigarette pack.*

Block Go-Carts

1134–1148 NORTH AMERICAN STREET

A large complex of block-deep buildings stretches from American Street westward to Bodine, just below Girard Avenue. These buildings can be identified as the former home of Block Go-Karts from the faint painted advertisements on the building walls. The business was operating out of this location in 1924. Prior to that, the buildings served as a baby carriage factory, as marked on city atlases from 1910. In 1875, these particular buildings did not exist and almost the whole block was part of a cotton mill. The buildings have been occupied for the last sixty-five years up to the present by Apex Fountains, a manufacturer of high-quality banquet, display and serving products, such as silver trays, fountain pieces and coffee urns, which still operates out of the buildings today.

The façade that faces American Street is uniform and neat and makes the grouping of buildings appear to be a single large warehouse. However, the façades on Bodine Street vary greatly from address to address in door height, window style, brick pattern and general architectural style. This suggests the complex was not built as a single unit but rather is a consolidation of smaller buildings, perhaps built independently and joined together at separate times. Smaller structures next to the building at the southern end have been demolished, adjacent to the horse stables and pasture of the present-day Philadelphia Trolley Works. It is here that we find the Block advertisements reappearing from under the stucco covering that has been hiding them for the past eighty-plus years. The signs can be found at both corners of the building—the edges facing Bodine and American Streets—but the Bodine Street sign is the more legible of the two and the one that is shown here.

We can easily read "BLOCK" at top, with another older sign appearing beneath it. Just below, we see "GO-CART...," any more of which is then obstructed from view by drain pipes and stucco. Just below that, we can make out "Every...," most likely the beginning of an advertising slogan or marketing claim, one we may know again, should time and weather have their way.

Supplee-Wills-Jones Milk Co.
1134–1148 NORTH AMERICAN STREET

This sign is one of those you notice one day and, despite its size, prominent placement and clarity, wonder why you'd never noticed it before. It's amazing that you still can find gems such as these hidden in plain sight.

On the corner of Fifth Street and Fairmount Avenue, on an expanse of uninterrupted brick wall above a single-story grocery store, we find a large painted mural advertisement. The ad features a tagline that reads, "By all means BUY... MILK" at the top and the product manufacturer's name "SUPPLEE WILLS-JONES" at the bottom. I had never noticed it before—perhaps the direction of traffic makes it difficult to see by car; it was only after walking south down the block against the direction of traffic one day that I finally noticed it.

The full tagline at top is most likely "By all means buy Gold Medal Milk," as seen in archive photos of other Supplee-Wills-Jones billboards in Philadelphia from the early 1920s. The lettering styles of both the tagline and the corporate logotype match up. Also consistent with other ads of the period is an area for illustration, typically of the head of a smiling cow, to the left of the composition, just below the tagline. While no trace of it remains visible here, the lack of lettering does suggest some sort of area reserved for something like an illustration. Whether it was a mascot or image of the product that was placed here in this particular ad is unfortunately unknown.

This was almost certainly a privilege sign, with other city archive photos from the 1950s showing a delicatessen in business at the corner store location below the sign.

L.H. Parke's Coffee Co.

FRONT BETWEEN GIRARD AVENUE AND WILDEY STREET

An old complex of buildings, this plot of land is illustrated in early atlases as a distillery, "whiskey brewery" and warehouse. An engraved datestone located on the Front Street side of the building reads, "HOPE MILLS 1848." Later maps have no record of what type of business (other than commercial) occupied the buildings at this location. Luckily, there are clues in the signage as to what happened here over the past hundred or so years

L.H. Parke Company started in 1889 as a partnership of Louis H. Parke and William P.M. Irwin. Their partnership took over the small pushcart business of Samuel Irwin, a veteran of the Civil War who had lost his arm in the Battle of Winchester, Virginia. Parke began in business as a seller of coffee, tea and spices. The merged company eventually grew to be a major

institutional wholesaler of canned goods and was famous for its "Unmatchable Dry Roast Coffees" and "Packed to Order" canned goods, spices, teas and coffees. In 1961, the company was sold to Consolidated Foods. At the time of the sale, the company was headquartered at this location in Philadelphia and had grown substantially to include offices and warehouses in Pittsburgh; Washington, D.C.; Richmond, Virginia; and Albany, New York.

The L.H. Parke building later served as a distributor warehouse and showroom for kitchen furniture and appliances. This explains some of the other signage found on other structures around the complex. For example, on the side of one of the larger of the buildings, we find "TAPPAN" with an image of a home cooking range in a lovely shade of yellow and "Appliances,

Cabinets, Vanities" on the opposite wall. Both of these signs are painted high up on the structure's walls, clearly visible from the elevated train tracks and station platform that straddles Front Street and Girard Avenue just a few yards away.

The Fruchter family, consisting of four brothers, their sister and their father, formed Adolph Fruchter and Sons, a wholesale kitchen firm, which in its heyday supplied many of the home and apartment complex builders that expanded the borders of Philadelphia through the period of rapid development immediately after World War II. Many of the fixtures and built-in furniture in residences of Greater Northeast Philadelphia can trace their original purchase back to this warehouse complex.

Today, there is a rather garish purple and white street-level paint scheme covering a portion of the building. It is obviously a modern addition. This might have been done to help brighten up the entrance, which sits below the shadows of the elevated SEPTA tracks. Painted lettering on the façade reads: "Fruchter Industries, Inc., Wholesale Distributors of Kitchens, Vanities & Appliances."

There are numerous overlapping signs around the complex, but peeking beneath all of them, you can still make out the words "PARKE'S COFFEE." The building has been vacant for decades now, and time, weather and vandalism are taking their toll. Much of the roofing and portions of walls have collapsed,

and much of the building that fronts Hope Street is badly damaged and in danger of collapsing further. The building itself is not secure, and access by vandals has been rather easy. Anti-graffiti efforts are attempting to solve some of the blighted appearance of the building by spraying large portions of the walls with brown paint. While mitigating the appearance of blight, this is also obscuring the old signage and advertisements as well. It seems that the signs may be covered over completely, or the buildings demolished, rather soon. Development is taking place everywhere around these structures, which may force something to happen here sooner rather than later. It would appear that these signs may not exist for much longer.

PHILADELPHIA'S RIVER WARDS are a group of neighborhoods that border the banks of the Delaware River. This particular area stretches from Vine Street at the southern end to the Frankford Creek at the northern end. The first settlers arrived here in the 1600s, and the population grew substantially with the arrival of European immigrants in the 1800s and early 1900s. The housing stock throughout these communities varies from the large mansions that line Girard Avenue to the tiny row homes that fill the small alleys and side streets, and, like the Northern Liberties to the southeast, manufacturing and industrial buildings are sprinkled throughout the gridded residential maze.

One of these neighborhoods has come to be known as "Fishtown." This name is derived from the area's former role as the center of the shad fishing industry on the Delaware River, although there has never been an official designation of this area with that name. Local legend also traces the origin of the nicknaming of Fishtown back to Charles Dickens, who visited the neighborhood in March 1842 and purportedly remarked on the high number of fishmongers clustered so close together. However, written records show this to be false, as the term had already been in use since at least the 1820s, a few decades prior to his visit.

In colonial times, most of what is considered to be the neighborhood of Port Richmond, and portions of the surrounding area to the northwest of Fishtown, was owned by Anthony Palmer, a colonial governor who had built up a substantial wealth from foreign trade. During the 1800s, with the invention of the coal-burning steam engine and subsequent adoption of this engine's use aboard ships, Port Richmond became a major shipping terminal, particularly for colliers, bulk cargo ships designed to carry coal. These ships received coal from the Reading Railroad facility at the port and transported it out to steamships at other locations. This industry continued until coal-powered steam engines were replaced by the more modern technology of oil and diesel engines around the end of World War I.

Both neighborhoods have been working class for centuries, with a large number of their inhabitants living within walking distance of their places of work. Many different kinds of industries flourished here due to the proximity of the shipyards, wharves and terminals that lined the riverfront, and with them came warehouses and structures that provided opportunities for advertising their wares and services.

RIGHT *A beautiful palimpsest, or layered overlapping, of signs at the former Eastern Candy Co.*

THE
RIVER
WARDS

Cramp Shipbuilding Machine Shop and Turret Shop

DELAWARE AVENUE AND SHACKAMAXON STREET

This square-shouldered, monolithic brick and glass structure once stood alongside the northbound lanes of Interstate 95 at the corner of North Delaware Avenue and Otis Street (now East Susquehanna Avenue). Long banks of paned, double-height windows hint at the soaring ceiling and the well-lit space within. This building was the last remaining structure of the once world-famous Cramp Shipyard.

William Cramp started his shipbuilding business in 1830 as the William Cramp and Sons Ship and Engine Building Company. This business would eventually become one of the world's largest manufacturers of iron ships. It was Fishtown's biggest employer well into the mid-twentieth century; the company employed generations of families and brought well-deserved fame to the neighborhood.

William Cramp's family had built its wealth through the fishing industry. The first ships Cramp made were wooden, but as technology changed, the Cramp company was able to follow suit. In fact, the Cramp company was the only American ship company that successfully transitioned from the manufacture of wooden-hulled ships to metal-hulled ships.

The earliest of these new metal ships produced at the shipyard were the "New Ironsides" built for the Union during the Civil War. Business at Cramp boomed again during World War I, when it helped build many of the impressive battleships in Teddy Roosevelt's Great White Fleet. It was this naval fleet that put America on the map as a world superpower.

As business slowed between the wars, the Cramp shipyard was purchased by the American Ship & Commerce Corporation in 1919. American closed the yard a few years later in 1927, once it became known that fewer ships were to be ordered by the U.S. Navy after passage of the Naval Limitations Treaty of 1923. But with the outbreak of World War II, the navy spent $22 million to reopen the yard as "Cramp Shipbuilding Company" to build cruisers and submarines in 1940. After fulfilling these duties, Cramp closed for good after the conclusion of the war in 1947. Slowly but surely, the structures were demolished, with just this single building remaining. Portions of it were removed to make way for the interstate, and it was shortened at its northeastern end.

Over the years, I remember the building being shortened and losing more and more ancillary buildings around it. A few other structures from the Cramp Shipyard complex still stood at the time I started photographing signs, most of them in the large lot across the street from the machine and turret shop. Sadly, I no longer have any photos of those other buildings, which were nothing more than partially collapsed shells. Soon after photographing them, they were razed and the complex left a huge vacant plot of land.

Under a thick coat of black paint, we can still see the hand-painted lettering of the words "Cramp Shipbuilding Machine Shops" present on the building. These signs appeared above one of the two eastern-facing garage doors along Richmond Street. There is not much signage on the building, relative to its impressive mass. However, when you consider that the building was just part of a once sprawling complex of numerous buildings and structures, many of which were much larger than this one, it makes sense that the signs are understated and less advertisement-like.

In May 2006, the current owners of the building drew up plans to renovate and convert the structure into condominiums. However, the Pennsylvania Department of Transportation's plans to reconfigure the Girard Avenue interchange of I-95 called for the building's demolition. Officials say that while the building was deemed to be a "contributing resource" to the Fishtown Historic District, sparing its demolition and leaving it in place would require the highway expansion to go west, directly into the residential neighborhoods, rather than east toward the river and into much less populated areas. And so it was decided; demolition of the building occurred in 2010.

LEFT *This is a shot of the long Richmond Street side of the Cramp Shipbuilding Machine Shop and Turret Shop as seen in March 2007. This building, the last of the once sprawling shipbuilding complex, met the wrecking ball in 2010.*

EDWARD CORNER

ROPE

CANVAS COVERS

BLOCKS and FALLS

BOAT and SHIP SUPPLIES

BLASTING MAT

WE BUY OLD ROPE

Edward Corner Marine Merchandize Warehouse

DELAWARE AVENUE AND SHACKAMAXON STREET

The Edward Corner Marine Merchandize Warehouse is one of the last surviving relics of Fishtown's once very close association with the maritime industry. It is probably one of the better-known examples of faded advertisements in Philadelphia, but its long-term vacancy and proximity to new developments along the riverfront, particularly the Sugar House Casino directly across the street, threaten its continued existence. The empty lots surrounding the warehouse have already been cleared and resurfaced for use as additional parking for the casino. On a recent trip to the site, I discovered a "Coming Soon" billboard had been erected in front of the building, complete with architectural renderings of a proposed development coming soon to the property. It seems that this remnant of Fishtown's seafaring past may not be here with us much longer.

Businessman Edward Corner purchased this plot of land on Shackamaxon Street sometime around 1882. Whether there was another building here on this lot prior to that is not known. On the present structure, a stone quoin facing Delaware Avenue reads "1921 E.C.," the date that Edward Corner (his initials) erected this building. This building would be fronting the edge of the newly widened Delaware Avenue when its construction was complete. Another stone quoin is located on the side that faces Shackamaxon Street and is dated 1870, possibly the year that Corner began to conduct his business here in Philadelphia. His marine supply business occupied this structure until 1960, when it was sold and converted into a furniture warehouse. It is currently vacant and boarded up.

Portions of the first story have been covered over in stucco, either to preserve the brick from further deterioration or to prevent graffiti, and it obscures some of the signage. Other signs have been partially painted over or covered with newer signs on wooden and metal panels. These are now slowly reappearing from beneath as the newer paint fades and the dilapidated sign panels fall off. The main advertisement of interest is a large mural that covers most of the northeasterly facing wall. Well composed and considered, the sign lists the items in which Corner's business specialized: "Rope and Canvas," "Anchors and Chains," "Canvas Covers," "Boat Supplies," "New and Used Rope," "Blocks and Falls," "Blasting Mats" and, finally, "We Buy Old Rope." Of particular note is an illustration of a pointing hand at the rear corner of the building, where Allen Street meets Shackamaxon, which faces traffic headed east to the Delaware. The words above the illustrated hand helpfully advise that "This is Edward Corner's Warehouse, Entrance at the corner."

Eastern Candy Co.
1125 EAST COLUMBIA AVENUE

LEFT *A beautiful palimpsest, or layered overlapping, of signs. There were at least three different signs for three different companies that were located here at one time. The latest and most visible of which is "The Eastern Candy Company," followed by "Penn Carpet Cleaning Co." and, finally, a third, which is unintelligible save for the beginning letter "Q."*

INSET RIGHT *Visible in the background of this 1956 photo.* **Photo courtesy of PhillyHistory. org, a project of the Philadelphia Department of Records.**

On an unassuming building in the middle of a residential city block, there sat a great palimpsest of overlapping signs. There are at least three distinct signs visible on this wall, the latest and most immediately legible of which was "The Eastern Candy Company." Eastern was a family confection company run by Nishan Androyan, who filed for incorporation in 1922. From newspaper clippings and obituaries, the company seems to have been in business here until the mid-1960s. There is not much in terms of records for the company other than some legal documents.

The sign is clearly visible in the background of this 1956 photo, which was taken from about a block farther west on Columbia Avenue. Here we can make out the brand name of candy for which Eastern was known: "Home of Tas-Tee Sweets."

Signage continued on the front of the building, where the signboard read, "Eastern Candy." However, peeking out beneath this sign we can see "CLEANING." An 1895 atlas shows this property as a carpet cleaning business and names it in the 1910 atlas as the "Penn Carpet Cleaning Co."

The building has recently been renovated into loft-style condos, and unfortunately, the signage has been altered. The large sign on the side of the building has been covered over with stucco, along with the rest of the wall and the ground story that faces

Columbia Avenue. The lettering on the front signboard has been painted over with a new blue and white signboard in an attempt to emulate the signage style of the day, somewhat unsuccessfully. The development has been named the Candy Factory, a nod to its most recent industrial occupant.

I used to live about a block away from this building, just off Columbia, and I found this particular assemblage of lettering to be particularly beautiful. I've used it for numerous projects, including imagery for which to market this book. I even included this image in a show on ghost signs held at the Primer Gallery. I think it captures the essence of why I love these types of signs: the historical interest, the mystery and the simple beauty in the patina.

Spruance Quality Paints

RICHMOND AND TIOGA STREETS

LEFT *Both sides of this row home feature large painted illustrations of products made by the Spruance company. This one, the larger of the two, features a paint or varnish can illustration, with the taglines "Ask Your Dealer" and "Sold by Leading Stores." Both ads were given a covering of green paint to obscure them from view, but they slowly began reappearing until they were demolished in early 2012.*

The Gilbert Spruance Co. was founded in 1906 at this complex of buildings on Richmond Street. The company manufactured paints, industrial coatings and wood finishes on site for the furniture and kitchen cabinet industries, a number of which were located in the immediate area. It was a family-run business that lasted until 1984, when it ran into trouble with the Environmental Protection Agency.

The New Jersey–based vendor that had been hired to handle Spruance's waste material removal was caught dumping at what eventually would become a number of Superfund sites. According to the law, Spruance was liable for part of the cleanup bill, even though it was not directly involved with the criminal dumping act. Facing mounting legal fees, the loss of its insurance coverage and bank loans and wave after wave of regulatory lawsuits, the owner was eventually forced to sell the Spruance business. Gryphin Coatings resumed production of paint and varnishes once it purchased the Spruance name, equipment and property in 1994. However, Gryphin also inherited the cleanup issues. By 2008, it was also forced to put the site up for sale, citing the inability to pay the EPA for the continued Superfund cleanup costs. The buildings sat vacant after Gryphin shuttered the plant, and after a few years of neglect, the entire complex was razed in early 2012.

One of the more prominent features of the complex was this brownstone row home, sitting by itself, separated and somewhat detached from the rest of the complex by the shipping yard. Demolition of the homes on either side of this row home to make way for plant expansion had opened up an opportunity for advertising. The blank brick walls on both sides of the building eventually featured large murals of painted illustrations of Spruance products. The larger of the two murals, photographed here in 2008, features a paint or varnish can illustration, with the taglines "Ask Your Dealer" and "Sold by Leading Stores" above and below. A similar but smaller ad appeared on the other side of the row home. Both ads were given a covering of green paint to obscure them from view at some point, but they had slowly begun to reappear from under the paint right up until the time they were demolished.

Siemon & Sons Barrels.

FRONT AND PALMER STREETS

Here, again, we find a handful of signs that, because of their placement, are difficult to notice in our day-to-day travels around the neighborhood. However, once you see these types of signs, you wonder how you went about your business without ever seeing them in the first place.

A decorative "H. Siemon & Sons Manufacturers of Barrels" has been painted at the top pediment of this former factory building. There are more faintly visible signs at the top corners on the sides of building that read, "H. Siemon & Sons New Barrels." These signs, while not easily seen from the street, are positioned to be visible from the elevated train that runs right in front of the structure. A simple and much less interestingly composed signboard identifies the business at street level.

The business is listed as a new member in the *National Cooper's Journal* in 1918, as manufacturers and dealers of barrels located at 2219 North Second Street. Today, this address is a vacant lot.

Long vacant, this large building has recently been converted into event space. The current tenants have kept and actually uncovered more of the original signage and plan to preserve and uncover whatever signs they find hiding behind the paint and stucco.

INSET RIGHT *An archive photo, commissioned by the Jackson-Cross Real Estate Company and taken circa 1940, depicting the large brick warehouse of H. Siemon & Sons Barrels. Note the clarity of the signs, especially the small ads high on the corners of the building, which have all but disappeared completely today.*

THE CITY BEGINS to fan out as it sprawls northward away from is historical center, and the tight confines of the gridded streets begin to loosen up. Scales shift in even greater degrees, as factories and warehouse buildings grow to enormous proportions, free from the constraints of the congested residential areas closer to the center of the city.

In colonial times, as with Port Richmond, most of this area was owned by Anthony Palmer, the colonial governor who established the small suburban town of Kensington in this location in the 1730s. It's interesting, however, that even to this day, Kensington is not a clearly defined area. Since the town has long since been incorporated into the city proper, sometime in the mid-1800s, its borders will probably never be officially agreed upon.

North Philadelphia is another puzzling name for a neighborhood with disputed boundaries. Technically, everything north of Market Street can be considered to be located in North Philadelphia, but the general acceptance is that the southernmost boundary is somewhere between Vine Street and Spring Garden Street. This large neighborhood is sandwiched between West Philadelphia and Germantown to the west and Kensington and Northeast Philadelphia to the east.

In the nineteenth century, both of these regions were considered to be among the leading centers of the textile industry in the United States, particularly in carpet manufacture. In 1880, over eight hundred textile firms employed over fifty thousand workers here. But industry of all sorts took up residence in these neighborhoods. For example, in 1870, there were a total of sixty-nine breweries located within the city limits, and most of those were found within these two neighborhoods.

Deindustrialization eventually took hold in the 1950s, as it did in most rust belt cities with a strong heritage in manufacturing. This led to significant population loss, high unemployment and economic decline. That economic decline led to the subsequent abandoning of homes, factories, warehouses and other businesses. As such, even today, these neighborhoods are a mix of housing, operating small industries, abandoned structures and vacant lots.

Neglect is, in some ways, a means of preservation. Many industrial sites here remain, strikingly, in almost exactly the same shape as they were left the day their doors were closed. Architectural details, signage and advertising remain as they once did, whereas, if located elsewhere, they may not have survived development or demolition. Hopefully there is a chance that someday a few of these structures, and their signs and advertisements, can be restored to their former glory.

RIGHT *"If it's H-O..." A fading painted advertisement for a once popular brand of oatmeal.*

KENSINGTON AND NORTH PHILLY

Orinoka Mills

2753 RUTH STREET

This large complex, just north of the Reading Railroad tracks in Kensington, contains a number of five-story brick buildings built between 1890 and 1920. The Solomon Brothers began the mills in the early 1880s as B.L. Solomon's Sons. By the 1890s, this operation featured eighty-five looms for the making of silk upholstery and curtain materials. Curtain production was halted in 1898, and instead the company refocused solely on designing and manufacturing fabric for furniture coverings.

James H. Clarke, a former superintendent for the company during the 1890s, became president of the Orinoka Mills in the early twentieth century. By 1913, three hundred looms were used to produce silk, wool, worsted and cotton upholstery here. The mill became known for producing highly specialized and intricate textile designs and constructions, with a high level of quality that rivaled fine fabrics found in Europe.

However, by the 1930s, the weaving operations were moved to York, Pennsylvania, and to locations in the South. The company would maintain offices here at this location in Kensington, as well as in Center City, Philadelphia, along with a small number of dyeing, finishing and warehouse facilities. In the 1980s, the firm moved outside the city to Horsham, Pennsylvania. Lantal Textiles, Inc. purchased Orinoka Mills and inherited its fabric collection archive, which dates back to the later part of the nineteenth century. Lantal now uses the Orinoka name as a registered trademark, and that name is now associated with the line of these archival fabric patterns.

The main sign on the Ruth Street building, which looked out west over the Reading Railroad tracks and toward the center of the city, was one of simple lettering. The repainting of the sign over different periods and the subsequent fading of those signs produced an interesting effect on the lettering, as the slight offset in alignment was revealed over time. Originally, manufacturing took place here, but the company kept its offices in Center City, hence the need to display "Philadelphia Office 1200 Chestnut Street" on the large sign. The company also had offices in New York City and Baltimore, Maryland, at one time.

Although some independent textile and manufacturing businesses still operate in the newer buildings of the Orinoka Mills complex, most of the older buildings had suffered serious deterioration after having been left vacant for more than a decade. Over the years, the structures had been losing brick, cornices and other features, sometimes falling onto the street below from many stories up. The City of Philadelphia condemned part of the structure due to this falling brickwork and demolished the older half of the mill building on Ruth Street in the summer of 2011. Unfortunately, this is the portion of the building that featured this Orinoka Mill painted sign.

Kolb's Pan-Dandy Bread
FIFTH STREET AND MONTGOMERY AVENUE

The Kolb Bakery appears in local signs and painted advertisements as far back as 1908. The baking company was listed in the 1909 Philadelphia city directory as doing business in three locations throughout the city: Tenth and Reed Streets, Broad and Butler Streets and Fifty-sixth and Market Streets. In an advertisement in the *Reading Eagle* dated March 4, 1911, we are given a little insight into what made Pan-Dandy Bread uniquely special:

> *"PAN-DANDY" is a bread made from the very highest grade of flour, purest of lard and sugar, and also contains as one of its principal ingredients "Malt Extract" which is used for the purpose of giving added value to the strength-building qualities of this bread.*

Although this sign is somewhat faint and appears to have been covered completely with a coat of red paint at one time, a few features still can be discovered. The Kolb's script can be seen prominently despite the weathering. From there, interpreting the sign is just a matter of some research. In archival images that feature other full Kolb Bakery painted wall advertisements, we find many of the same trapezoidal composition elements present in this sign, as well as the baker figure illustration (which in this example is barely visible at the far left), with those of Kolb's Pan-Dandy Bread. Unfortunately, a recently painted band of graffiti covered up in brick-red paint has obscured whatever other messaging exists below the huge "PAN DANDY" lettering.

This large ad is clearly a privilege sign, with the business name advertised above the Kolb's script, squeezed in a narrow band along the roofline: "J. NUTALL. Dealer in New & Second Hand Machinery." There is similar lettering on signboards painted across the front of buildings that face Fifth Street.

The opposite wall of the building, looking south down Fifth Street, is a palimpsest of signage. The most prominent of this advertising reads, "Nutall Machinery" in a few different iterations, overlaying older illegible signage. A smaller, more modern and more illustrative "Signs" ad appears below these larger ads, but it is difficult to

make anything else out, save for the last few digits of a phone number at the bottom of the ad.

I love this sign just because of the sheer size of its calligraphic letterforms. It was amazing to arrive at this street corner and be presented with something of this scale. And the building itself is covered on almost all sides with interesting signage and advertising from different periods. This was truly an interesting find.

If It's H-O...

AMBER AND WESTMORELAND STREETS

The H-O Cereal Company (originally Hornby's Oats, hence the initials of H-O) was a New York company that formed in the Bronx in 1893 and later moved its facilities to Buffalo in 1895. The company manufactured two different types of oat cereals. It competed directly with such well-known brands as Quaker and General Mills. From small beginnings and after gaining additional brand name product lines through acquisitions, the company and its plants grew. It was fully modernized during World War II in order to supply the United States and Allied forces with cereals. After the war ended, the company continued its growth, and during the 1950s, H-O was producing over six thousand cases of cereal per day.

But increased competition and internal economic troubles eventually forced the company to sell the business to competitors. By 1975, the cereal plant had closed and was followed by the closing of the remaining milling operation in 1983. The Buffalo plant, which after being sold was used as a tire warehouse, suffered a massive fire in 1987 and was then left vacant. In 2006, the plant was demolished to make way for a new casino development project.

This advertisement, located at the corner of Amber and Westmoreland Streets, was most likely a privilege sign for the business that used to exist on this corner. Most atlases have the modern structure housing a soap factory up until the mid-'60s, which does not necessarily tie to the ad, but a spur of the Pennsylvania Railroad passes by just two blocks away. This line services several nearby warehouses, including immense ones built for the receiving and storage of goods for food retailers.

H-O often employed interesting "plain talk" advertising slogans, such as "Steam cooked—that's why" and the like. Brown paint has been used to cover up the graffiti on the building, but unfortunately it also covers the rest of the advertisement. I was unable to find an example from archival H-O advertisements with a slogan that exactly matches this layout and phrasing, so perhaps we'll never know what this ad's complete tagline once said.

Gretz Beer

GERMANTOWN AVENUE AND OXFORD STREET

LEFT *The Gretz smokestack, located atop the brewery complex, advertising Gretz beer to all of North Philadelphia. The brewery was busy from the 1880s all the way up until the 1960s, with only a short break while it was closed during Prohibition.*

Philadelphia has a centuries-old tradition of brewing, dating back to at least 1680, when city founder William Penn began work on his own brewery here in the early settlement. America's founding fathers wrote the Declaration of Independence and the Constitution in the rowdy taverns of the colony—even the U.S. Marine Corps was conceived, according to legend, at a long-gone tavern in what is now Society Hill. The first brewing of lager beer in America happened here in the Northern Liberties in 1840.

As I mentioned previously, by 1870, there were sixty-nine separate breweries that were making beer in Philadelphia. An entire section on the western side of the city was called Brewerytown, where a collection of fourteen breweries were crammed together within a nine-block industrial neighborhood. Those few blocks alone were responsible for supplying half of the city's output of beer.

But Prohibition shuttered all the breweries—at least on paper, though some attempted to stay open illegally. Many of the smaller facilities simply closed their doors and stopped producing beer altogether. While many more attempted to reopen after the repeal of the law in 1933, some had lost too much in revenue and just could not sufficiently recover. Competition was fierce, and national conglomerates began to be too much competition for the smaller local establishments. The last of the city's old breweries, Schmidt's, closed for good in 1987.

Rieger and Gretz was founded in 1881, and the brewery complex was built at the intersection of Germantown Avenue and Oxford Street. Along with some of its local counterparts, Rieger and Gretz did reopen after Prohibition ended. However, the Riegers' involvement in the brewing business came to an end, and the brewery spent the next twenty-eight years renamed as the William Gretz Brewing Company. The Gretz smokestack, located atop the brewery, proudly displays the "Gretz beer" lettering in a sharp mid-'30s style.

Due to increasing competition from both local breweries and the national giants, Gretz ceased operations and closed down the brewery complex in 1961. The building has remained vacant since, but there are movements to save the beautiful and ornate structures. There is hope that the complex will be restored to the height of its beer-producing condition sometime soon.

Peter Woll & Sons Mfg. Co. Curled Hair, Feather

BERKS STREET AT HANCOCK STREET

LEFT *A faded sign for "PAPER" can be seen lettered vertically over the much older "PETER WOLL & SONS FEATHER CO" sign. The height of this tower allows for the sign to be seen for many blocks in all directions, ideally from the main traffic and railroad thoroughfare of American Street a few blocks away to the west.*

This is an interesting sign, not just because of its size or lettering style but because of the nature of the business that it advertises. Curled hair manufacturers took the refuse from tanneries, morocco (a dried insect–dyed leather made from goatskin) factories and slaughterhouses and repurposed it into useful products. This refuse was everything the tannery or butchery could not use, such as hair, feathers, entrails and organs of butchered animals. These materials were made into products like scrub brushes or glue. An unpleasant business, surely, but profitable, since there was a constant supply of the raw material and a definite business in its disposal or reuse.

Case in point, this family firm has been working in the curled hair business for well over 125 years; it has been in business from 1880 right up to the present day. Structures on both sides of this stretch of Berks Street still display painted signs advertising the family name and occupation, although the businesses moved out from these buildings decades ago.

The Woll name has been displayed on the five-story brick building on the north side of Berks Street from 1891 on. Architectural details of the building, such as the corner towers, make it seem like a much newer structure, but the building outlines conform to insurance atlases from the 1890s, as well as an illustration of the building in a print advertisement placed by the firm circa 1895.

In 1916, Peter Woll and Son were joined by Woll and Sons, Feather Company, at 169 Berks Street. By 1922, a city atlas shows the firm had moved to the corner of Berks and Mascher Streets, about a half block away. By 1945, its former buildings were occupied by other companies. The larger building eventually became a paper warehouse, and today it is home to the Globe Paper Company. A faded sign for "PAPER" can be seen lettered vertically on the water tower painted above the much older "PETER WOLL & SONS FEATHER CO" sign.

The low, one-story building across the street is unusual for the area; it may have had one or more stories removed or built on the site of a demolished building or group of buildings. It still wears the full "Peter Woll & Sons Mfg. Co. Curled Hair" sign painted in large lettering down the length of the Berks Street façade. There are signs on the Mascher Street side for later businesses: Rapid Electric and Penn Scale manufacturing companies. Both were listed in a city industrial directory from 1944.

LEFT *This smaller one-story building of the two family businesses on Berks Street still proudly wears the full "Peter Woll & Sons Mfg. Co. Curled Hair" sign painted in large lettering. This sign is nearly the length of the building.*

Hope Machine Co.

SECOND AND DAUPHIN STREETS

Imagine stumbling across this garage for the first time. When viewed in a modern context, it seems almost unbelievable. Hope Machine? Steam engines? It all just seems too surreal. Even I, who can look at this stuff with a bit of detachment, was at first concerned that perhaps this was too good to be a real sign. That perhaps, like the B. Schapiro and Bros. sign in Old City, this sign too could have been painted in modern times to simulate faded advertising. Maybe as a backdrop for some movie or television show set? Surely something this interesting, this cool, could not be real?

After some digging around through archived business directories, I was pleased to discover that, yes, the Hope Machine Company, presumably named for nearby Hope Street, had been listed in the industrial directories of Pennsylvania as far back as 1919. The company placed an ad under the "contract work" section in the Automotive Industries of New York directory in 1918. Therefore, this was a company that actually existed, these signs are authentic and aged and the company actually did once perform the work these signs advertised.

The main sign above garage doors reads, "HOPE MACHINE CO. Engineers and Machinists" and has an interesting effect similar to that of the old Orinoka Mills sign—numerous repaints followed by that paint fading over time that reveals the words to be slightly off alignment. The smaller signs read, at left, "Automobiles Repaired" and, at right, "Steam & Gas Engines Repaired." This particular stretch of Second Street, near the intersection of Dauphin Street, still houses a few automobile repair shops and sales lots, indicating that the automotive industry has had a presence here since the earliest days of motoring.

Much like the Eastern Candy sign, I've used an image of this particular sign for numerous projects, including some of the imagery to market this book. I have also included this image in an exhibition on ghost signs held at the Primer Gallery. This sign helps make a tangible yet magic connection from the modern world to a distant past, and it is simply amazing.

LEFT *This sign features beautiful and clear lettering, which reads "HOPE MACHINE CO. Engineers and Machinists." The sign harkens back to the very earliest days of motoring, when the brass-era horseless carriage was still a novelty and hardly the commonplace convenience we take for granted today. Still seems almost too interesting to be an actual period sign.*

The Schlichter Jute & Cordage Co., Sterling Paper

2155 CASTOR AVENUE

LEFT *The slogan "It takes a golden effort to make a Sterling product" used to be painted on either side of this factory's famously ornate clock tower. It is barely visible now under the many layers of advertisements that are slowly fading back into view. The Moorish-style clock tower was one of two towers surrounding the older portion of the complex. The other, slightly shorter tower, which featured a canopy but no clock, is no longer standing.*

This sign is one of those head scratchers. I know a few people who have seen the sign here and had no idea what was going on. It is a bit confusing, especially when nothing is known about the artwork here. It even took me a little bit of digging to finally get to the bottom of the story behind this unique and interesting project.

I was originally drawn to this site by what I thought was an interesting overlapping of historical signage. Upon closer observation, I realized the signage was not your typical signboard, nor was it a typical list of products or services painted in orderly fashion along the cornice lines of the building. The brick walls now inexplicably proclaim strange phrases such as "THERE IS NO CLOCK WHEN IT'S TIME TO FLY" and "WE WILL NEVER FORGET YOU" and "YOU TURN AROUND AND YOU COME BACK REMEMBER."

Sterling Paper Converted Paper and Paperboard Product Manufacturers, which was established 1973, seems to have been the most recent tenant of this long, massive building, and it still operates from the site. The signs that face Castor Avenue used to have the advertising slogan "It takes a golden effort to make a Sterling product" on either side of the famous clock tower. These slogans have been painted over with a Philadelphia Mural Arts project, but the older lettering can still be seen beneath.

In 2001, the president of Sterling Paper was looking to rehabilitate his fading and peeling signage. At his request, he commissioned a mural project for his factory building from the Philadelphia Mural Arts Program, the largest such public art program in the United States. The project involved artists from the Philadelphia Mural Arts interviewing the president about his past and recording the most notable statements from his stories. They then pulled some of the more memorable quotes from the interview and painted them in place on the building, in a fashion that was similar to the original signage.

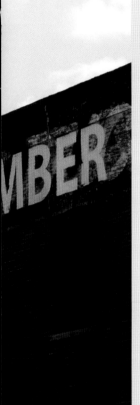

But if you travel around to the sides or rear of the building, farther away from the highly trafficked Castor Avenue and down the side streets of Coral and Butler, you can see the fading Sterling signage giving way to earlier signs and offering up a clue about the original inhabitants of the site.

City atlases from as early as 1875 show the ornate buildings and clock tower facing Castor Avenue in place and the buildings themselves titled "Aramingo Mills." However the entire area of land around the building is labeled "THE SCHLICHTER JUTE & CORDAGE CO." There are large painted signs on the rear (facing Butler Street) and sides (facing Coral Street) of the building that show that same name revealing itself from below the Sterling signs.

Jute is a long, soft, somewhat shiny vegetable fiber that can be spun into coarse, strong threads. Partially a textile fiber and partially wood, it is one of the most inexpensive natural fibers and is second only to cotton in the amount produced and the variety of its uses. It is very suitable for agricultural bulk packaging and helps make for good-quality industrial yarn, fabric and netting. You've most likely come across the material as potato or other vegetable sacks or as floor rugs. The similarity of jute and paperboard processing probably made this building an ideal site for a business such as Sterling to move into.

LEFT *Three layers of lettering appear on this long factory building, fading into one another and vying for attention: the Schlichter Jute & Cordage Co., Sterling Paper Co. and an interesting Philadelphia Mural Arts project featuring quotes from the Sterling Paper president and portraits of the Sterling family members.*

Walton Bros.

2131 NORTH AMERICAN STREET

LEFT *"Walton Bros. Grain" sign, facing south toward traffic traveling north on American Street. This sign has been partially obscured by the newer building next door. There are signs for other mills that occupied the building here, as well as a signboard painted in the style of the older signs for the current occupant.*

This is a sign I discovered by happy accident. I was looking for the location of the Art and Industry space, which had converted this former mill into a shared co-working space. Only after traveling north on American Street toward the building did I see the large "Walton Bros. Grain" on the south-facing wall, partially obscured by the newer buildings next door. I walked around the building, interested in the signage, and realized that this building was the location I had been looking for. There is additional signage on the building as well. The north-facing wall has the word "Office" with an illustrated hand pointing to the front of building, and there are numerous signboards along the front, which faces American Street.

The atlas of the city of Philadelphia from 1887 lists this business on this block as "Walton Bros. Hay & Straw" and, from 1910 through 1942, simply as "Feed House" or "Feed Whse." H.B. Cassel & Sons—a grain, straw, hay and mill feed dealer that was located here after the Walton Brothers—has also left its mark on the front of the structure. The first-story signboard and a sign at the top of the façade show faded traces of the Cassel name in lettering. The company suffered a huge fire in 1938, no doubt fueled by the highly combustible materials held in storage here. Descriptions and dramatic photos of the event were sensationalized in the period newspapers.

A new, modern and interesting Art and Industry signboard has been painted over the previously existing signboards, but it is appropriate in style and scale in relation to the original sign and the building overall. The reversed lettering style lets the original faded signage show through the negative space, which is a unique approach, and it is a very respectful gesture of the current tenants nodding to the historic nature of the building.

Livery and Boarding Stables

1200 BLOCK OF NORTH FOURTH STREET

LEFT *"Livery and Boarding Stables," painted in ornate black lettering over a white field vertically down the southern-facing edge of the building. The sign continues at the top of the wall along the roofline, but it is so badly weathered that it is impossible to make out any of the lettering.*

It's easy to forget in our modern age that prior to cars, subways, buses and trolleys, the primary source for the energy to do work and to transport people and goods from place to place was the horse.

As the city land became increasingly built up, pastures became smaller in size or disappeared altogether, especially the closer to the center of the city one was located. These animals needed a place for feeding and shelter, and thus boarding stables began to spring up where neighborhoods started to become more densely developed. These boarding stables were much more plentiful at the turn of the century. There are many of these types of structures left in the city, most long-since converted to other uses by this point. But there are a few still in use, chiefly by the tourist carriage companies, located throughout Callowhill, the Northern Liberties and in the southern parts of North Philadelphia, where we find the location of this brick stable.

The space is labeled as "LIVERY" on the 1910 atlas, but on an atlas from 1895, the space was an open marble yard, as the building had not yet been constructed. On atlases post-1910, the building is shown simply as a structure zoned for industrial use. It has been converted into residential units today.

The vertical signage on the edge facing south down Fourth Street toward Girard Avenue is faded, but the ornamental lettering is easily read: "Livery and Boarding Stables." The sign continues at the top of the wall along the roofline, most likely spelling out the stable name or providing some further advertising. However, the sign is so badly weathered that it is impossible to make any of the lettering at this point. Signage only exists on the southern-facing side of the building.

SOUTH PHILADELPHIA, known colloquially as South Philly, began like most other neighborhoods in the city: as a satellite town outside of Philadelphia proper. This town was composed of smaller townships, such as Moyamensing and Southwark, which, along with many of the other outlying suburban towns of the period, became part of the city officially with the passing of the Act of Consolidation in 1854.

During the Industrial Revolution, this neighborhood witnessed a rapid growth in population, in part due to immigration to the area from Ireland, Italy and other European countries. The area accommodated this influx of population with the continuance of row home architecture, a method of shared-wall home construction that was immensely popular at the time in England. However, developers here in Philadelphia took the process a step further. On speculation that the homes would easily sell, a developer would purchase an entire block of land plots, build a row of connected houses and then sell the finished buildings individually. Large undeveloped tracts of land in the city could be developed quickly and in the most efficient way possible by employing this method. This soon became the accepted standard when developing urban areas, not only here in Philadelphia but also across the country.

This regimented method of development created a seemingly endless grid of brick two- and three-story row homes, broken only by the crisscrossing of Passyunk and Moyamensing Avenues (ancient established Native American trails)

and the occasional square or park. It may have been off putting, perhaps even oppressive, at first glance. But the benefits of relatively affordable new home ownership, located on a street that was well paved, well lit and well drained, was for most families worth the monotony of repetition. Many street block corner buildings served as grocery or butcher stores that served the streets around them, and thus their flat façades offered prime surfaces for signage and advertisements targeted at the local population.

I grew up here in South Philly. Most of my life has been spent living in row homes. Most of my immediate family lived within walking distance of one another, and to some extent, they still do. I think my appreciation for this city, and cities in general, all started with the sense of tight-knit community that the neighborhood fostered. Neighbors actually knew their neighbors. Family lived within walking distance. You knew your butcher, grocer, barber and tailor by name. Something about the closeness and the uniqueness hidden within the uniformity gave me a sense of comfort and home that few places can match.

At a time when your family, friends and co-workers all lived around you and there was no such thing as public or personal transportation, the necessities of daily living were bought close at hand, and everything was nearby. You can understand this sense of microcosm reflected in the local advertising.

RIGHT *This icehouse was the last of three immense complexes in the Italian Market area, photographed the day before its' demolition.*

SOUTH
PHILLY

Kolb's Bread, Bond Bread and others

NINETEENTH AND CATHERINE STREETS

LEFT The side of an old storefront that featured a number of mural-sized privilege signs. Lettering for "Bond Bread," "Kolb's" and what appears to be "FRUIT HEART" intermingle with colorful but indistinguishable illustrations. This old structure has been demolished, and the sign along with it.

The history of Bond Bread can be traced back to 1911, when the General Baking Company was incorporated in New York as an amalgamation of nineteen other baking businesses. By 1930, General Baking owned fifty plants that supplied baked goods to cities in eighteen states. The baking of bread, the flagship product that was sold under the trade name of "Bond Bread," accounted for over 90 percent of sales, and at its peak, production averaged nearly one and a half million loaves of bread per day. That is a staggering amount considering the somewhat local nature of the business.

There were many competitors in the baking marketplace, and as smaller operations merged with others to become larger conglomerates, advertising played a big role in setting one company apart from all of the other available brands. Bond sponsored television programs, ran commercials, placed print ads in newspapers and magazines and commissioned privilege signs, such as this one, on the walls of neighborhood corner convenience stores and groceries.

By the early 1960s, General Baking was feeling the effects of the increased competition from other baking conglomerates, as well as large supermarkets, many of which had begun installing bakeries within their own stores. In addition, charges of illegally conspiring to fix bread prices in Philadelphia and New York City tarnished the brand's image, which in turn hurt sales. By 1972, the company had folded or sold off just about all of the Bond Bread baking division.

Interestingly, one of those bakeries in the original amalgamation of nineteen other baking businesses that composed General Baking was another local breadmaker, Kolb Bakery. And interestingly enough, we can see the Kolb's script from an older advertisement reappearing from beneath the Bond Bread sign.

At the time this photo was taken, not much was left of this Bond Bread ad except the white calligraphic lettering of the Bond logo. But even more faded advertisements appear on another layer; whether beneath and older, or above and more recently painted, is uncertain. We can make out "FRUIT HEART" in block lettering in the center and "BEST CHEWING GUM EVER" at bottom. There also appear to be numerous colorful illustrations, but they are too weathered to interpret.

I have a soft spot for South Philly corner stores. I have always loved their character—the hand-cranked patterned-fabric awnings, the small angled entrance doors with the ornamental iron post at the corner and the boxes of produce carefully put out for display every morning. Sadly, there are very few of these left, even fewer that have not been renovated or updated in some way. Unfortunately, this Bond Bread sign no longer exists, as the building it had been painted on was demolished in 2011, shortly after the photo was taken.

STANLEY'S LOANS
THIRTEENTH AND SNYDER STREETS

This sign is another one of my all-time favorites. It is located about halfway between the house I grew up in on Alder Street and my grandmother Gilda's house on Juniper Street, just a short twelve-block walk from one house to the other. This sign was on the way there and back. That route also happened to pass close to Italiano's, the water ice stand, which I appreciated very much and visited very often during the humid months of many Philly summers. For a time, I also attended A.S. Jenks public middle school one block away from this sign on Moyamensing Avenue, so I would see it often while growing up nearby.

The lettering on the façade of this building has been exposed like this for as long as I can remember, and as the years pass, the wonderful jumble of words just seem to become clearer and more prominent. The entire façade along Moyamensing Avenue is absolutely covered in faded advertisements and lettering, and the signage continues around the corner on Clarion Street. It's a shame that the ground story has been covered over in a generic sheet of red brick; it would be amazing to see what signs might have been painted at street level on the columns between what used to be the large glass expanses of shop windows.

Because it's difficult to read on the oblique angle, here is what the lettering is spelling out, from left to right:

Top row:
"...broke? Uncle Bill has plenty"

"Uncle Bill's Licensed and Bonded Pawn Brokers"

"Kodaks, Bicycles and Sporting Goods"

"Talking Machines, Musical Instruments and Sewing Machines"

The last two are too difficult to make out what is painted there.

Middle row:
"Money To Loan," flanked either side by yellow three globe pawn symbols.

Bottom Row:
"Store Orders Accepted"

"Men's and Boy's Clothing and Shoes"

"Diamonds, Watches and Precious Stones"

"Trunks, Bags and Suit Cases"

"Guns Revolvers"

LEFT *The entire façade of this uniquely shaped building, which at one time was a pawn shop, is covered in amazing decorative lettering. Signage appears on every surface. Some highlights: "Talking Machines, Musical Instruments and Sewing Machines," "Diamonds, Watches and Precious Stones" and "Guns Revolvers.".*

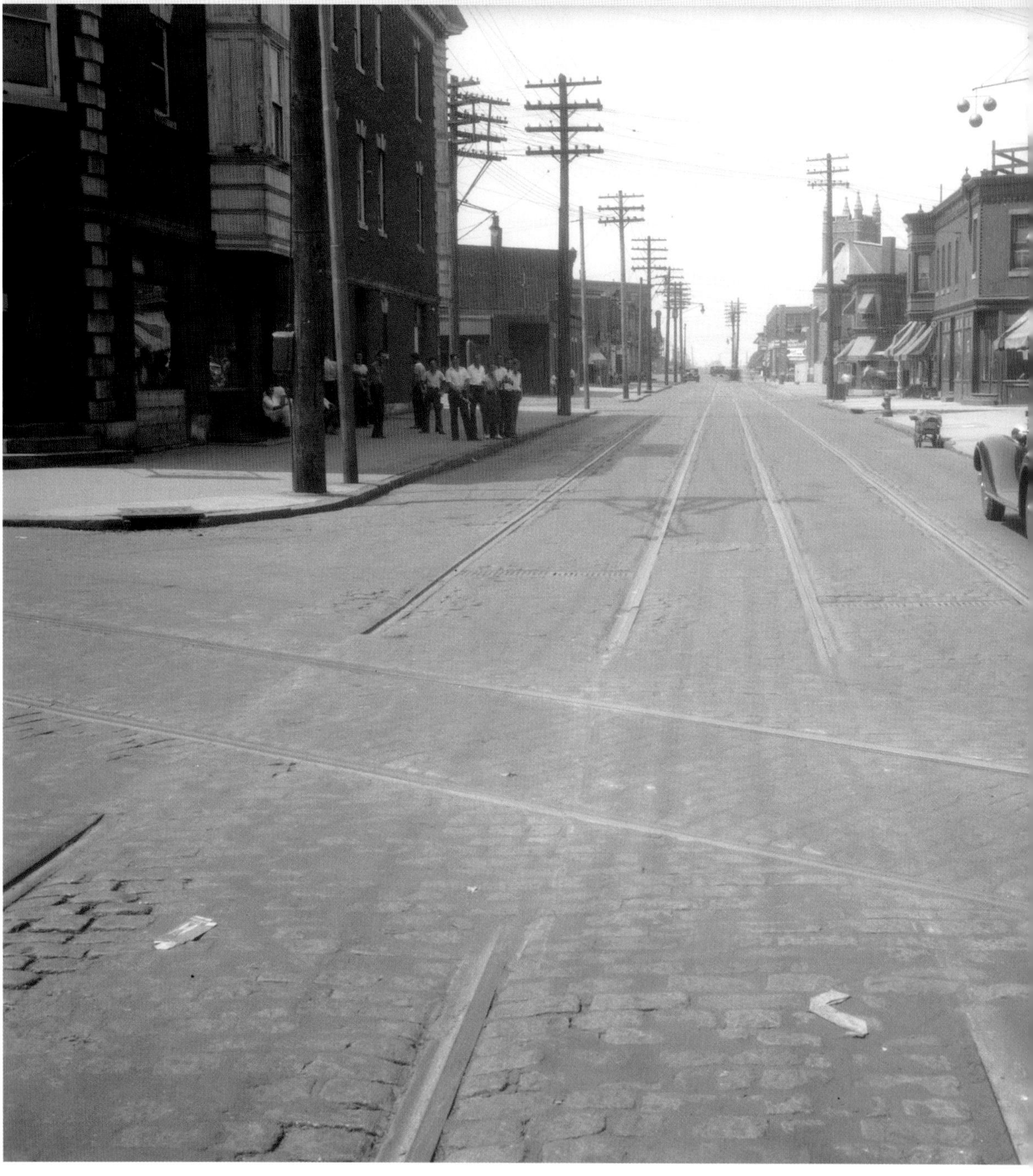

In my research I came across a city archive photo of the intersection of Moyamensing Avenue and Nineteenth Street, taken in 1935. The subject of the image is the street surfacing project and disused trolley tracks, as it was taken by the Public Works Department; it was most likely part of a before-and-after record of some street resurfacing or repair. You can clearly see the store in the upper right corner, with the multiple awnings, just above the roof of the parked car. The painted signage appears to be pretty much the same composition as today, albeit much clearer. There apparently was also a vertical sign with large letters (see the panels featuring the letters "L L S" dropping in from just off the top of the image) and a few metal dimensional pawn symbol signs hanging from the front of the store.

In this shot, we also become aware of how recent the phenomenon of automobile ownership is. Visiting this corner today, you would be hard-pressed to find a place to double-park, let alone find a space along the curb. As with other cities, personal car ownership was slow to take hold within the population, since so many necessities were local, and by this time public transportation systems had become efficient. The emptiness of the streets recalls a much simpler and quieter time.

LEFT *This city archive photo of Moyamensing Avenue was taken in 1935. The subject of the image was most likely the street surface and trolley tracks, but you can see the store in the upper-right corner, with the signage visible. There is even more painted signage present here than what is visible today.*
Photo courtesy of PhillyHistory. org, a project of the Philadelphia Department of Records.

Grand Theatre

SEVENTH AND SNYDER AVENUE

LEFT *"Grand Theatre—TALKIES—Matinee Daily." This original painted signage was (unintentionally) protected from much weathering by the elements by a covering of aluminum siding. This siding was part of the façade of "Bargain Stores," which occupied the theater after it closed. The siding was removed after partially collapsing in 2006 or 2007, once again revealing the faded lettering and reminding pedestrians that the space once used to be a movie theater.*

This is a sign that quite literally uncovered itself and one that many people have submitted to the blog because of its unique lettering. For years, this building had been covered in generic white aluminum siding, which was used to modernize the appearance of the building and to cover most of the movie theater's original façade. A few years ago, the siding that had covered the structure for decades started coming loose and falling off, revealing that most of the original painted signage beneath was still intact. And there it was, all this amazing signage, where the day before there had been none and on a structure where most people had forgotten a theater had once existed. It was another of those moments, much like the Hope Machine Co., where the sign seems just too interesting to be real.

The sign over the main Snyder Avenue entrance reads, "Grand Theatre—TALKIES—Matinee Daily." A sign over the Seventh Street entrance reads, "Grand Theatre—Direction." There are also other smaller painted signs around the top corners of the building.

Early sound films incorporating the sound of dialogue synchronized with the onscreen action—known as "talking pictures" or "talkies"—were a technological marvel at the time of their introduction. Any theater with the equipment to show such films would be eager to advertise such a wonderful advancement. But at some point, probably as the term grew out of fashion, the painted lettering spelling "TALKIES" on the front of this theater was painted over in black, to hide it against the (then) black background of the sign. It was forgotten about until the background black paint, which did not have the layer of lead paint below it, all but faded away, revealing the "TALKIES" lettering once again.

The Grand Theater was originally built as the Synder Avenue Baptist Church in the late 1800s. As the neighborhood changed before World War I, the building changed from a place of worship and became an event hall before it was eventually converted into a movie house in 1911. At first, the house projected silent films, and those shows were joined by vaudeville acts. The introduction of movies with sound most likely prompted the advertisement of "TALKIES" prominently on the front of the theater.

Another renovation, by architect W.H. Lee, took place in the 1930s. The Grand had 850 seats and one screen and was able to charge a little more than other local theaters because it featured an air-conditioned theater. As the age of inner-city movie theaters declined and the public started frequenting newer, larger cineplexes in the suburbs, the Grand stopped showing films. It eventually closed, and a retail clothing store took over the space by the mid-1960s. Those tenants had placed the white aluminum siding over the façade.

American Ice Company

NINTH AND WASHINGTON AVENUE

This icehouse was one of three immense complexes that used to call the Italian Market area their home. Dating back well over one hundred years—it was listed on 1875 city atlases as the Knickerbocker Ice Company—the massive, nearly block-long edifice was the final remaining warehouse of its kind and stood as a constant reminder of a time before the era of refrigeration, even an era before electricity was commonplace.

During this era, coal and ice would arrive from the waterfront via train tracks that ran down Washington Avenue. The large loads would be deposited in the warehouse space and divided into smaller deliveries. The iceman would then deliver large blocks of ice daily via a horse-drawn carriage (and later in a truck) to businesses and homes in the area. Chunks of ice would be chiseled off by hand to fit within each customer's individual home icebox. The American Ice and Coal Company also supplied many of Philadelphia's once-numerous local breweries with ice to keep their brewed products cold while in storage and transit. Similarly, coal carriages and trucks ran down the alleys behind homes, delivering coal through chutes that emptied directly into bins in row house cellars. Some row homes still have these chutes, or at least the remainders of the interior delivery end, in their basement walls.

Abandoned for forty years and left to the ravages of the weather, the interior of this main icehouse structure was so deteriorated that the building was deemed beyond repair and could not be

rehabilitated. The Redevelopment Authority designated the blocks around the icehouse "blighted" in order to condemn the building. The complex was demolished in January 2008 and, along with it, these painted signs. While there were plans to construct a new senior living center on the site, as of this writing, the location remains a vacant lot awaiting development.

Street Cleaning Wagon Shop
TWENTY-FIFTH STREET AND OAKFORD STREET

ABOVE *This simple but elegantly designed brick building has a well-considered painted sign at the very top of its cornice. Lettering reads: "DEPT. OF PUBLIC WORKS WAGON SHOP, BUREAU OF STREET CLEANING."*

This handsome sign features very carefully composed lettering and layout that reads: "DEPT. OF PUBLIC WORKS WAGON SHOP, BUREAU OF STREET CLEANING."

This warehouse is a uniform, rather stately looking brick shed that is nearly half a block long. There is very little signage on the structure—or anything else, really—that could be seen easily. Before the construction of the railroad viaduct directly in front of the building between 1926 and 1928, this building and this sign marked the presence of the city's "responsive, efficient, modern government" in action in the neighborhood. The lettering of the sign proudly heralded the work being done here to service the public.

Unfortunately, once the wide train viaduct was constructed, the sign was blocked from most views by the concrete skeleton of the tracks. The sign remains intact to this day, and the building is in remarkably original shape, occupied with some sort of light industry.

THE POPULATION of West Philadelphia grew substantially after World War I and throughout the first half of the twentieth century. This was due in large part to the horsecar (later replaced by the motorized streetcar) and the Schuylkill River bridges that allowed residents to commute to and from Center City for work, while still living in a more peaceful, country-like environment. As such, West Philadelphia became one of the earliest streetcar suburbs.

The westernmost portion of the neighborhood was once home to some of the most expensive real estate in the country, and many of the fine and stately examples of Victorian-era architecture remain. However, the area has been in a slow yet steady decline over the past few decades, due in part to a significant portion of the middle- and upper-class residents leaving the area and moving either farther west to the suburbs or to other sections of the city.

Manayunk is a neighborhood in the northwestern section of the city, located along the banks of the Schuylkill River. The original settlement, which was known as Flat Rock in the early 1800s, became widely renowned for the construction of a dam, canal and locks along the river. The canal project was the first of its kind begun in the United States.

The area's name was eventually changed to one that comes from the language of the native Lenape Indians; their word for river was *manaiung*, which literally translated to "a place to drink." In the 1820s, the establishment of water-powered mills and factories increased dramatically, and the area became known as a manufacturing village. Manayunk continued to be one of the manufacturing centers of Philadelphia for the next one hundred years.

Manayunk in particular has enjoyed a sort of renaissance, with industry giving way to shops and restaurants. The neighborhood still retains a certain small village sort of charm. West Philadelphia has also enjoyed a sort of renaissance, with the expansion of universities and hospital complexes in the area attracting students and families as well as related businesses. Both areas are rich in history and have interesting wall advertisements to be discovered.

RIGHT *Detail of the Reading Anthracite Company logos (circular in shape and with the tagline "Famous Anthracite") at the corners of the Hare and Cute Coal Pockets.*

WEST PHILLY AND MANAYUNK

John Decker & Son

2702 WEST GIRARD AVENUE

John Decker was a successful manufacturer of sheet metal roofing and cornices for sale to the architectural trade in Philadelphia. His nephew was William Decker, the architect of many of the brewery buildings and homes of prominent brewers in the nearby Brewerytown neighborhood. William had worked with the Decker family sheet metal company from the 1870s. It is very likely that William assisted in the overall design of the family's contracting headquarters and metal fabrication shop here at this location.

The building where John Decker had his business still stands on Girard Avenue. The structure is topped with an impressive story-high cornice, emblazoned with dimensional lettering touting the business's wares and services, accented with golden highlights. At the very top center of the cornice, which even today towers high above any neighboring building, reads the date of 1891, the year in which the sheet metal factory was established.

This cornice, and in fact the entire front of the mixed architectural–style building, functions as an advertisement for the business. While the ground floor has been converted into a modern and rather featureless storefront, the rest of the building is intact and is covered in full-size examples of many of the architectural details the business had on offer for the customer. It functioned as an amazing display of all of the building fashions and technologies available at

the close of the nineteenth century, from window styles to masonry finals and balustrades. The dimensional lettering on the sign reads, "Architectural Sheet Metal Works," "Tin Roofing, Copper Cornices" and "Metallic Sky-Lights."

Although the street-level storefront has been renovated and modernized, the rest of the building remains intact, and today, we can still marvel at this interesting combination of architectural styles and artistic flourishes. The sign seems to be well kept, as it has recently been repainted and retouched. Thankfully, someone recognizes the significance of the building's features and is working to actively preserve them.

LEFT *This amazing story-high metal cornice—and, in fact, the entire front of this building—functions as an advertisement for the John Decker metal stamping business. It is covered in full-size examples of its architectural offerings, from window styles to finals and balustrades. The dimensional tin lettering reads, "Architectural Sheet Metal Works," "Tin Roofing, Copper Cornices" and "Metallic Sky-Lights."*

7UP

FIFTIETH AND LANCASTER STREETS

You might look at a 7UP sign and think that it couldn't possibly be that old. The brand does seem to be decidedly youthful, much newer and younger than some other soda brands, probably because it doesn't rely on its heritage as part of its advertising strategy. Nonetheless, it seems odd to find such a seemingly modern mark fading away as a privilege sign on the side of an abandoned storefront. However, that's exactly what is found here. We can roughly calculate the age of this sign based on clues from the design characteristics of the logo and with surprising results.

The popular lemon-lime-flavored soft drink that eventually came to be known as 7UP was created by Charles Leiper Grigg in October 1929, two weeks before the Wall Street stock market crash that signaled the start of the Great Depression. Yet despite such ill timing, and with some tweaking of the product's name (it was originally called "Bib-Label Lithiated Lemon-Lime Soda"), the product caught on as a popular alternative to contemporary colas and other fruit-flavored drinks. Nobody quite knows the exact origin of the name 7UP, but its iconic name and simple logo have become an inextricable part of American culture.

The earliest design of the 7UP logo sported wings, very much like the winded feet of the god Mercury. However, this artwork was not used for very long. The design used through the 1930s to the 1950s features the 7UP lettering in white, outlined in dark green, all over a red background. The red dot, or spot, was not introduced as a graphic device until the mid-1960s. Therefore, we know that this sign dates between the mid- to late 1930s to the early 1960s, at the latest. City archive photos of the property from the early 1950s show that there are definitely signs painted or posted here, but the angle doesn't afford a view of what those signs say.

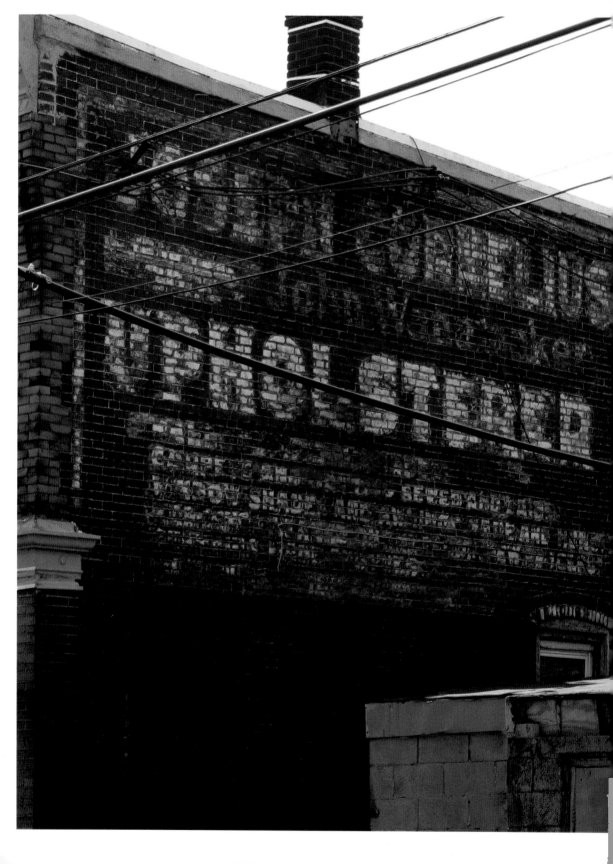

Joseph Cornelius, Upholsterer

FIFTIETH AND LANCASTER STREETS

This sign is located about a half block off the main shopping street district along Baltimore Avenue and faces the wide intersection at Cedar Park. The sign is painted on a wall at the end of a block of row homes that run next to a narrow alleyway. The end building seems to have been a storefront of some kind; even though it has been renovated and altered, the columns and walls on either side are original, making it different than the homes attached at left, which all feature columned porches. City atlases show the structure as a mixed-used commercial and residential property as far back as 1910.

The storefront here perhaps housed the retail shop of "Joseph Cornelius, John Wanamaker Upholsterer" at one time. I was unable to find any information on Mr. Cornelius or what his relationship was with John Wanamaker or the world-famous Philadelphia department store.

The Wanamaker dry goods and clothing store, called the John Wanamaker & Co. "Grand Depot," as it was converted into a store from a railroad depot in 1875, was one of the first and best-known department stores. One can assume that Joseph Cornelius was either an employee of importance at Wanamaker's or a manufacturer who sold his wares there.

Very little can be made from the lines of lettering at the bottom of this sign, beneath the large UPHOLSTERER letters. Just a few words from the second and third lines can be deciphered: "CARPETS AND...SEWED AND LAID" and "WINDOW SHADES AND AWNINGS MADE AND HUNG."

Uneeda Biscuit

FIFTY-FOURTH AND MARKET STREETS

LEFT *A very faded privilege sign for Uneeda Biscuit, a 110-year-old brand from the National Biscuit Company (whose name was eventually combined and shortened to the now more familiar Nabisco). The Uneeda Biscuit was the first cracker to be sold in a freshness-sealed wax and cardboard package, instead of individually from barrels.*

As mentioned previously with both Kolb's and Bond Breads, bakeries throughout the country went through a period of regional consolidation in the late nineteenth and early twentieth centuries. They merged into companies such as Chicago's American Biscuit and Manufacturing Company, the New York Biscuit Company and the United States Baking Company. In 1898, the National Biscuit Company was formed from the combination of the three just mentioned; this particular merger resulted in a company with 114 bakeries across the United States and with headquarters in New York City. The "biscuit" in the name of the company is a British and early American English term for cracker-like products.

After the consolidation, the president of the National Biscuit Company challenged his new company employees to create a package that would result in the distribution of fresher products. This paved its way for In-Er Seal package, which was a system of inter-folded wax paper wrappers within a cardboard box, designed to repel moisture and fight staleness by sealing in the freshness of the contents. National Biscuit created a new cracker that was flakier and lighter than any of its competitors' versions and could remain so for a lengthy period of time due to this new packaging system. This new product was given the name Uneeda Biscuit and was the first to employ the new In-Er Seal packaging when it was introduced in 1898.

Up until that point, crackers were usually sold in bulk, unbranded and packed loosely in barrels. Mothers would give their children a paper bag and ask them to visit the corner store to have the bag filled with crackers. National Biscuit used this then common image as part of the Uneeda Biscuit advertising artwork, which depicts a boy carrying a pack of Uneeda Biscuit in the rain. In 2009— amazingly, right up to the modern day, after over 110 years on neighborhood grocery store shelves—Nabisco discontinued the Uneeda Biscuit line, as the product was no longer profitable.

In the advertisement mentioned above, we can pretty clearly make out the "Uneeda Biscuit" lettering. Unfortunately, what is below that lettering has been covered over by a band of thick brown paint in an attempt to cover up graffiti. What is above the "Uneeda Biscuit" lettering is also somewhat of a mystery, although by comparing this ad's composition with that of other Uneeda Biscuit painted wall advertisements, we can determine there most likely was not any sort of illustration outside of a logo for NBC. We can make out a yellow border and a lettering style that are both consistent with signs of the era. There is a different panel at the top, above the Uneeda sign, outlined in white, which may have been the name of the business whose wall the ad is painted on, all but confirming that this was a privilege sign.

Hare and Cute Coal Pockets

JAMESTOWN AND CRESSON STREETS

Coal pockets, once a common sight along railroad tracks and industrial areas within cities, were basically areas that branched off the main railroad line for coal yards to receive, unload and store loads of coal from railcars. The Hare and Cute pocket could accommodate loads of up to three fifty-five-ton railroad hopper cars. Coal was unloaded from the cars and separated into large bins, which funneled down to an opening at the bottom; coal could then be dropped to the street level for either loading for delivery or direct retail sale from underneath the bins. There are street-level garage-like bays beneath each bin, each with its own set of doors, that would allow a horse-drawn cart or truck to pull in to receive coal directly to their cargo areas. At the time of the construction of these Manayunk pockets, dealers were selling mostly to local homes and area small businesses.

The metal shed, built circa 1929, is located just off the main elevated tracks above Jamestown and Cresson Streets. Few enclosed coal pockets like the Hare and Cute remain standing along the Reading Railroad lines. This one is a short spur that has a concrete foundation, topped by a pitched-roof shed that is constructed from corrugated metal. The roof was designed to keep out rain and snow, which during the winter months could freeze otherwise exposed coal, making it difficult to separate and use.

There are two sets of painted advertising lettering present on the side of the metal shed. An older sign for Hare and Cute is visible, much darker and rusted. Hare and Cute was succeeded by James Cute and Sons. One can distinctly make out each name's unique set of lettering overlapping the other. Reading Anthracite Company logos (circular in shape and with the tagline "Famous Anthracite") flank the large letters on either end of the structure.

The shed itself has long been in disuse and disrepair. However, the grounds around the structure are open and now used as a parking lot. The property had been fenced off prior to its conversion into parking spaces, but there were multiple access points along the dilapidated iron gate that permitted entry. I had the chance, many years ago in my college days, to get onto the property and into the concrete foundation section below the shed. Amazingly, sitting in each bay were the original coal delivery trucks, as if they had just been parked for the night, although a bit dilapidated from decades of neglect.

From the design of the chrome grilles and Chevrolet insignia, I've determined these trucks were built sometime between 1941 and 1946. It's hard to be more precise, as the models changed very little due to the outbreak of World War II, which limited production of civilian trucks. When I visited a few years later, the trucks were gone. Recently, the bays have been covered over with modern metal garage doors.

LEFT *The unique Hare and Cute coal pocket structure. Here you can see the metal shed as it sits atop the concrete dispensing bays. Hopper cars would pull in from the right and dispense their loads into the bins below. The two names of the company (at the time of construction, it was Hare and Cute, then with change in ownership became James Cute and Sons) are both visible. Also note the two painted Reading Anthracite logos on either end of the metal shed, with lettering that reads "Famous Anthracite."*

Epilogue

FOR THE BETTER PART of two centuries, the hand letterer's craft had been indispensable to the advertising trade. As new technologies emerged, commercial art saw the unfortunate demise of this time-honored skill. The evolution of technology, however, brought upon us a new era of signage: supergraphics. Things could be made larger, faster and cheaper than ever before and in ways never before possible. Hand painting fell out of fashion, no match for the inexpensiveness and absolute precision of computer-generated artwork.

Sign painting may no longer be the dominant method for advertising, but it is far from a dead form of communication. The painstaking and time-consuming process of hand lettering and sign painting still resonates with people. During this time of economic uncertainty, people are beginning to look at the way they consume. They are considering ways of making their dollars go further, and they expect the things they invest in to last longer and be of higher quality. More conscious consumption is affecting all businesses and therefore reshaping the advertising, marketing and messaging that companies are putting forth. By revisiting the past, people are learning that quality and craftsmanship are values that trump quick and cheap. People are rediscovering the benefits of doing things in a traditional, well-practiced manner and that nostalgia and retro are trumped by timelessness and quality. There is something to the adage "They don't make them the way they used to."

We're seeing this in the rise of the popularity of all things Americana, the resurrection and celebration of old brands and products that bring with them that sense of timelessness, a comfort in being tried and true. Some of the more iconic advertising campaigns of recent times have touched upon these sentiments—Levi's "Go Forth" campaign by Wieden+Kennedy immediately comes to mind—and hand lettering has helped lend just enough of that authentic truth to these campaigns.

We are also experiencing a time when art and design has come to the mainstream forefront. Companies and brands are now expected to incorporate design into every aspect of their business. A brand is no longer just a mark on a product—it is how it communicates with its users or consumers, the attitude and essence it exudes, the actions it takes and the way it cohabitates with consumers. Companies that hold design to a high standard and embrace it in every part of their commerce are ones that have managed to flourish in this age. Apple, Target, Nike and Coca-Cola are just a few examples of companies that embrace and champion design that immediately spring to mind.

Within the area of design, typography in particular has been enjoying a renaissance. As technology advances, it starts to blend seamlessly into our everyday lives. There is a movement to soften and humanize technology and our constant digital flow of information. With the advent of higher-resolution screens on devices and the application of typefaces to websites and online content, the general public is beginning to appreciate and expect information that is designed and crafted to suit their tastes and expectations of the brand or service with whom they are communicating.

Hand lettering was, and still is, that interesting intersection of commerce and art. It has a much closer connection with pure artistic creation than other forms of graphic design and therefore a more approachable and interesting aspect to it. Street art, once considered mere acts of vandalism, has matured into a recognized art movement. Graffiti has moved from back alleys and subway cars into art galleries and from galleries into popular culture. Artists who are looking into different techniques and lettering styles are looking back into the old methods of hand lettering and painting styles and incorporating that into their work.

A prime example of just such an artist is Steven Powers, who wrote a short opening foreword to this book. Powers is a Philadelphia native and a working New York City studio artist. He also at one time wrote graffiti in Philadelphia and New York under the name ESPO. While his early work blurred the line between legal and illegal, his recent professional work is rooted in sign painting and its technique. A number of his projects are at the scale and in the location of signage as it was originally practiced. "A Love Letter for You" was a collaboration by Powers with the City of Philadelphia Mural Arts Program, sponsored by the Pew Center for Arts & Heritage. This project in Philadelphia, about the complexities and rewards of relationships, celebrates the sign painter style and features lettering murals that are painted high on building walls to be seen from the elevated public transportation train tracks. This project has spawned similar works in Brooklyn, Syracuse and Coney Island.

It is also a time when people are moving back into cities and finding their way back into areas that have been underpopulated and long forgotten. As development happens and neighborhoods change, more and more people are discovering signs such as these and coming face to face with the past in a new and unexpected way. I have been getting a lot of questions and e-mails of support on the blog recently and a most definitely positive growth in readership.

So, at a time of pessimism and bleakness, perhaps these small, colorful glimpses into the past can serve as reminders for us, reminders of the hard work of those who have gone before us and the truth that lies in the perseverance of their work. Perhaps we can gain some inspiration from their hard-learned techniques and the celebration of the considered, well-crafted, beautiful things they made. Perhaps in looking back at where we were, we can get a better sense of who we are today and where we're going.

Bibliography

"About John Evans' Sons, Inc.: History." http://www.springcompany.com/Company_Intro.htm#History. Accessed 30 April 2012.

"About Momentum." Momentum Worldwide. http://www.momentumww.com/#/about. Accessed 19 September 2012.

"About Nathan Trotter: Our Past." http://www.nathantrotter.com/about.htm. Accessed 30 April 2012.

"About O-Cedar." http://www.ocedar.com/about-ocedar. Accessed 30 April 2012.

"About PhillyHistory.org." http://phillyhistory.org/PhotoArchive/StaticContent.aspx?page=About. Internet. Accessed 30 April 2012.

"About Us: History." National Chemical Laboratories. http://www.nclonline.com/history.php. Accessed 19 September 2012.

Adam Steinmetz Steam Marble Works Trade Card. Courtesy of the Winterthur Library, Joseph Downs Collection of Manuscripts and Printed Ephemera.

"Advertising Century: Timeline." A 295-Year Synopsis of the Most Important Events in American Advertising, 1704 to 1999. http://adage.com/article/special-report-the-advertising-century/ad-age-advertising-century-timeline/143661.

Around the World in Eighty Days. IMDB.com [movie database website]. http://www.imdb.com/title/tt0048960. Accessed 19 September 2012.

Bailyn, Bernard. "Nathan Trotter: Philadelphia Merchant, 1787–1853." *Business History Review* 29, no. 4 (December 1955).

"Billboard." *Wikipedia*. http://en.*Wikipedia*.org/wiki/Billboard. Accessed 30 March 2012.

Bonsall, Joseph H., and Samuel L. Smedley. *Atlas of the City of Philadelphia, 1862*. Philadelphia: J.B. Lippincott & Co., 1862. Map Collection of the Free Library of Philadelphia.

"Botany 500." *Wikipedia*. http://en.*Wikipedia*.org/wiki/Botany_500. Accessed 30 April 2012.

Boyd, William Henry. *Boyd's Blue Book: A Directory from Selected Streets of Philadelphia and Surroundings*. Philadelphia: C.E. Howe Company, 1891.

"Brownstone of the Day: John Decker & Sons Sheet Metal Works." *Philly Brownstoner*. No longer available. Accessed 15 November 2010.

Bunn, Don. "History, Chevrolet Trucks: Segment Four: 1941–1946 Art Deco Pickups." Pickuptrucks.com. http://www.pickuptrucks.com/html/history/chev_segment4.html. Accessed 30 April 2012.

Catalogue of copyright entries: Pamphlets, leaflets, contributions to newspapers or periodicals, etc.; lectures, sermons, addresses for oral delivery; dramatic compositions; maps; motion pictures, Volume 14, Issue 2. Library of Congress, Copyright Office, 1917.

Chilton Co. *The Iron Age, Volume 103, Part 1*. New York: Iron Age Publishing Co., 1919.

Claus, R.J., and K.E. Claus. "A Brief History of the Sign Industry." *Signs of the Times Magazine* (September 1976).

"Collier (ship)." *Wikipedia*. http://en.*Wikipedia*.org/wiki/Collier_(ship_type). Accessed 30 April 2012.

Cox, Robert M., Jr. "Superfund Destroys a Small Business: Liable For Cleanup Whether Guilty Or Not." *PERC Reports* 21, no.1 (March 2003).

"Cramps machine shop." PlanPhilly. http://planphilly.com/node/928. Accessed 30 April 2012.

"Cunningham Piano Company." *Wikipedia*. http://en.*Wikipedia*.org/wiki/Cunningham_Piano_Company. Accessed 30 April 2012.

"The Cunningham Tradition." http://www.cunninghampiano.com/history/. Accessed 30 April 2012.

Defebaugh, Edgar Harvey. *Barrel and Box and Packages, Volume 23*. Chicago: Lumber Buyers' Publishing Corporation, March 1918.

———. *Barrel and Box and Packages, Volume 26*. Chicago: Lumber Buyers' Publishing Corporation, 1921.

Detweiler, Margit. "13 Histories: Blasts from the Past Along Center City's Back Street." *Philadelphia City Paper*. http://archives.citypaper.net/articles/112797/cov.13.side.shtml. Accessed 1 July 2011.

"DPW, Bureau of Street Cleaning Wagon Shop." *Necessity for Ruins*. http://ruins.wordpress.com/2009/03/24/dpw-bureau-of-street-cleaning-wagon-shop/. Accessed 30 April 2012.

Dreitlein, S.C. "The Philadelphia Row House: America's First Row House." *Row House Magazine*. http://www.rowhouse-magazine.com/featuredHomes/featuredRows_phillyRows.html. Accessed 30 April 2012.

"Edward Corner Marine Warehouse." *PlanPhilly*. http://planphilly.com/node/1749. Accessed 30 April 2012.

"Elder and Jenks: History." http://www.elderandjenks.com. Accessed 30 April 2012.

"Esslinger's Little Man Ale: circa 1940." *Rustycans.com*. http://www.rustycans.com/COM/month0803.html. Accessed 17 February 2008.

Evans, B.R. [Benjamin Ridgway]. *Dallett's Old Soap Manufactory, Northeast Corner Tenth and Callowhill Streets, 1884.*[graphic] Philadelphia: B.R. Evans, 1884.

Evans Sign Company. "History of Signs." http://evanssigns.com/history.htm. Accessed 30 March 2012.

"Firms & Offices/John A. Roebling's Sons Company." *Nicola Janberg's Structurae, International Database and Gallery of Structures*. http://en.structurae.de/firms/data/index.cfm?id=f000169. Accessed 30 April 2012.

"Fishtown, Philadelphia, Pennsylvania." *Wikipedia*. http://en.*Wikipedia*.org/wiki/Fishtown,_Philadelphia,_Pennsylvania. Accessed 30 April 2012.

Freedley, Edwin Troxell. *Philadelphia and Its Manufactures: A Hand-book Exhibiting the Development, Variety, and Statistics of the Manufacturing Industry of Philadelphia in 1857. Together with Sketches of Remarkable Manufactories; and a List of Articles Now Made in Philadelphia*. Philadelphia: Edward Young, 1859.

"Freire Charter School: About Us: Welcome, Head of School." http://freirecharterschool.org. Accessed 30 April 2012.

Fritsch, Paul R. "The Sign has Oldest Experience Table In Advertising." *Signs of the Times Magazine* (February 1947).

F. Weber advertisement. *Arts & Decoration Magazine* 14 (November 1920).

Gates, Kellie Patrick. "How One Shipbuilder Impacted Philadelphia and the World." *PlanPhilly*. http://planphilly.com/how-one-shipbuilder-impacted-philadelphia-and-world. Accessed 16 September 2010.

"General Host Corporation." *Funding Universe*. http://www.fundinguniverse.com/company-histories/General-Host-Corporation-company-History.html. Accessed 30 April 2012.

"General Marine's History." http://www.generalmarine.org/about.html. Accessed 19 September 2012.

Gennaro, Lorraine. "Crushed Ice." *South Philly Review*. http://www.southphillyreview.com/news/crushed_ice-73787072.html. Accessed 30 April 2012.

———. "Ice Capades." *South Philly Review*. http://www. southphillyreview.com/news/ice_capades-73758427. html. Accessed 30 April 2012.

Genovese, Peter. "Ghost Signs: Jersey's Commercial History Is Written Large in Faded Paint on City Buildings." *Star-Ledger*. http://www.nj.com/news/index. ssf/2012/03/ghost_signs_jerseys_commercial.html. Accessed 30 March 2012.

"Googie Architecture." *Wikipedia*. http://en.*Wikipedia*. org/wiki/Googie_architecture. Internet. Accessed 30 April 2012.

"Grain Elevators, A History." *Buffalo History Works*. http://www.buffalohistoryworks.com/grain/history/ history.htm. Accessed 30 April 2012.

"Grand Theater." *Cinema Treasures*. http:// cinematreasures.org/theaters/4911. Accessed 30 April 2012.

"Hair Singeing." *HairFinder.com*. http://www.hairfinder. com/hair3/hair-singeing.htm. Accessed 30 April 2012.

"Harold Prince." *Wikipedia*. http://en.*Wikipedia*.org/wiki/ Harold_Prince. Accessed 30 April 2012.

Hexamer, Ernest, and William Locher. Philadelphia and Surrounding Area Atlas Collection. Hexamer & Locher, 1858–1860. Map Collection of the Free Library of Philadelphia.

Historical Society of Pennsylvania. "American Coal and Ice Company Ice House." *Phila Place*. http://www. philaplace.org/story/187. Accessed 30 April 2012.

———. "G.A. Bisler Paper Boxes Building/Liberties Lofts Apartments." *Phila Place*. http://www.philaplace.org/ story/210/. Accessed 30 April 2012.

"History of Premier Malt Products." http://www. premiermalt.com/our.history.html. Accessed 4 January 2009.

"The History of Wilbur Chocolate." http://www. wilburbuds.com/docs/history.html. Accessed 30 April 2012.

"H. Leonard Fruchter, 85, Kitchen Supplier, Teacher." http://www.jewishexponent.com/article/16474/H_ Leonard_Fruchter_85_Kitchen/. Accessed 4 January 2009.

Hopkins, G.M. City Atlas of Philadelphia, Vol. 6, Wards 2 through 20, 29 and 31. Philadelphia: G.M. Hopkins & Co., 1875. Private Collection of Matthew Ainslee.

Hull, Callie. Industrial Research Laboratories of the United States, *Bulletin of the National Research Council (U.S.)*. Washington DC: The National Research Council, The National Academy of Science, 1946.

"Improvement in Baggage Transfers." *Philadelphia Times*. 1 May 1886. S 30 April 2012.

Irwin, Don. *L.H. PARKE COMPANY: Pushcart to a Multi-Million Dollar Corporation*. Philadelphia: Irwin Family History Book, November 2011, revised January 2012.

"J.E. Berkowitz Company History." http://www. jeberkowitz.com/company/details/history.aspx. Accessed 30 April 2012.

"John A. Roebling." *Wikipedia*. http://en.*Wikipedia*.org/ wiki/John_A._Roebling%27s_Sons_Company. Accessed 30 April 2012.

"John Wanamaker." *Wikipedia*. http://en.*Wikipedia*.org/ wiki/John_Wanamaker. Accessed 30 April 2012.

Jump, Frank. *Fading Ads of New York City*. Charleston, SC: The History Press, 2011.

"Jute." *Wikipedia*. http://en.*Wikipedia*.org/wiki/Jute. Accessed 30 April 2012.

"Kensington District, Pennsylvania." *Wikipedia*. http://en.*Wikipedia*.org/wiki/Kensington_District,_ Pennsylvania. Accessed 30 April 2012.

"Kensington, Philadelphia, Pennsylvania." *Wikipedia*. http://en.*Wikipedia*.org/wiki/Kensington,_Philadelphia,_ Pennsylvania. Accessed 30 April 2012.

Klein, Michael. "Church of Scientology Buys Site in Center City. It Has Purchased More Spacious Quarters on Chestnut Street and Plans to Expand." *Philadelphia Inquirer*, 1 July 2007.

Kolb's Pan-Dandy contest advertisement. *Reading Eagle*, 4 March 1911.

Kostelni, Natalie. "Society Hill Furniture Store Closes, Family Sells Building." *Philadelphia Business Journal*. http://www.bizjournals.com/philadelphia/stories/2008/03/10/story6.html. Accessed 30 April 2012.

"Lantal: The Company: Orinoka." http://www.lantal.ch/index.cfm?ID=A0A0282A-1CC4-875D-BDCD93C306EDB818. Accessed 30 April 2012.

Leech, Ben. "Unlisted: Schlichter Jute Cordage Works." *Field Notes from the Preservation Alliance for Greater Philadelphia*. http://fieldnotesphilly.wordpress.com/2010/07/30/schlichter/. Accessed 30 April 2012.

"List of Pennsylvania Breweries." *Wikipedia*. http://en.*Wikipedia*.org/wiki/List_of_Pennsylvania_breweries. Accessed 30 April 2012.

"A Love Letter for You." http://www.aloveletterforyou.com. Accessed 19 September 2012.

Ludwig, Corinna. "Rudolph Wurlitzer (1831–1914)." *Immigrant Entrepreneurship; German-American Business Biographies*. http://www.immigrantentrepreneurship.org/entry.php?rec=45. Accessed 30 April 2012.

"Manayunk, Philadelphia, Pennsylvania." *Wikipedia*. http://en.*Wikipedia*.org/wiki/Manayunk,_Philadelphia,_Pennsylvania. Accessed 30 April 2012.

Miller, Fredric M., Morris J. Vogel and Allen F. Davis. *Still Philadelphia: A Photographic History, 1890–1940*. Philadelphia: Temple University Press, 1983.

Mosher, Bruce. "NJ Private Express Companies." *Journal of the New Jersey Postal History Society*. http://njpostalhistory.org/media/archive/162-may06njph.pdf. Accessed 30 April 2012.

"Nabisco." *Wikipedia*. http://en.*Wikipedia*.org/wiki/Nabisco. Accessed 30 April 2012.

The National Cooper's Journal 34 (May 1918).

"The New And Old Entwined The Building's Character Counts for Many Tenants." *Philadelphia Inquirer* [article online]. http://articles.philly.com/2000-12-08/news/25578749_1_ceilings-historic-building-tenants. Accessed 30 April 2012.

"Orinoka Mills Corporation." *Wikipedia*. http://en.*Wikipedia*.org/wiki/Orinoka_Mills_Corporation. Accessed 30 April 2012.

"Pabst Brewing Company." *Wikipedia*. http://en.*Wikipedia*.org/wiki/Pabst_Brewing_Company. Accessed 4 January 2009.

Philadelphia Belting Company. *Superbelt Delivers the Full Horsepower*. Philadelphia Belting Company, 1917.

"Philadelphia Ghost Signage Project Gets Inked." *Fading Ad Blog*. http://www.fadingad.com/fadingadblog/?p=635. Accessed November 16, 2007.

Philadelphia Mural Arts Program. http://muralarts.org/about. Accessed 30 April 2012.

"Piano Activities in Philadelphia." *Presto-Times*, 5 May 1928.

"Port_Richmond, Philadelphia, Pennsylvania" *Wikipedia*. http://en.*Wikipedia*.org/wiki/Port_Richmond,_Philadelphia,_Pennsylvania. Accessed 30 April 2012.

"Prince Music Theater." *Cinema Treasures*. http://cinematreasures.org/theaters/1803. Accessed 30 April 2012.

The Reference Register for General Business Reference. New York: White, Orr & Company, 1918.

"Rehab Begins on Girard Warehouses." *PlanPhilly*. http://planphilly.com/node/2144. Accessed 30 April 2012.

Robert L. Latimer & Co. Manufacturers and Dealers in Bolting Cloth, Mill Machinery, and Mill Furnishings. Philadelphia: Evans Print House, 1900.

Roush, Chris. "Hidden Treasure—An Unopened Package of Cigarettes from 1910." *T206 Museum*. http://www.t206museum.com/page/periodical_81.html. Accessed 18 February 2008.

Rubin, Dan. "Looking Up for Ghosts of Philly's Past." *Philadelphia Inquirer*, 14 November 2007.

Scardino, Albert. "New Yorkers & Co.; Oatmeal Maker Hires Santa For a Battle With 2 Goliaths." *New York Times*. http://www.nytimes.com/1987/12/21/business/new-yorkers-co-oatmeal-maker-hires-santa-for-a-battle-with-2-goliaths.html. Accessed 30 April 2012.

Schenck, Helene, and Parrington, Michael. *Workshop of the World—A Selective Guide to the Industrial Archeology of Philadelphia*. Wallingford, PA: Oliver Evans Press, 1990.

Scranton, Philip. *Proprietary Capitalism: The Textile Manufacture at Philadelphia, 1800-1885*. Cambridge, UK: Cambridge University Press, 2003.

"7Up." *Snopes*. http://www.snopes.com/business/names/7up.asp. Accessed 30 April 2012.

"7 Up (United States)." *Wikia Logopedia*. http://logos.wikia.com/wiki/7_Up_(United_States). Accessed 30 April 2012.

"Sign Painting." *Wikipedia*. http://en.*Wikipedia*.org/wiki/Sign_painting. Accessed 30 March 2012.

"Signs of Early Times." *Signs of the Times Magazine*, April 1940.

"Singe." *Wikipedia*. http://en.*Wikipedia*.org/wiki/Singe. Accessed 30 April 2012.

Smith, Sabra. "Foto Friday: Signs of the Times." *My Own Time Machine*. http://myowntimemachine.com/2011/07/01/foto-friday-signs-of-the-times/. Accessed 1 July 2011.

"Sound Film." *Wikipedia*. http://en.*Wikipedia*.org/wiki/Sound_film. Accessed 30 April 2012.

"South Philadelphia." *Wikipedia*. http://en.*Wikipedia*.org/wiki/South_Philadelphia. Accessed 30 April 2012.

Spina, Laura M., and Karen Chin. *The Old City Historic District, A Guide for Property Owners*. Philadelphia: Philadelphia Historical Commission, 2009.

Stage, William, and Arthur Krim. *Ghost Signs: Brick Wall Signs in America*. July 1, 1989. St. Louis, MO: Floppinfish Publishing, July 1, 1989.

"Steve Powers (artist)." *Wikipedia*. http://en.*Wikipedia*.org/wiki/Steve_Powers_(artist). Accessed 19 September 2012.

Supplee-Wills-Jones Milk Co. advertisement. *Billboard Magazine*. Nielsen Business Media, Inc. 21 January 1950.

Telleria, Abby. "The Chocolate Works Apartments." *Multifamily Executive* 17 (January 2007).

"Theater History." Prince Music Theater. http://princemusictheater.org/our-theater/theater-history. Accessed 30 April 2012.

Thomas, Adam. *Apparitions of the Past, The Ghost Signs of Fort Collins, An Historical Context*. Report submitted July 2007 to the Advance Planning Department, City of Fort Collins, Colorado.

"US Foods: Early History." *Wikipedia*. http://en.*Wikipedia*.org/wiki/US_Foods#Early_history. Accessed 30 April 2012.

Wallace, Ethan. "Look Down!" *Hidden City Philadelphia*. http://hiddencityphila.org/2011/10/6957/. Accessed 25 October 2011.

"Walldog." *Wikipedia*. http://en.*Wikipedia*.org/wiki/Walldog. Accessed 30 April 2012.

Washington, George, and Walter S. Bromley. *Atlas of the City of Philadelphia, 1895*. Philadelphia: G.W. Bromley & Co. Anthanaeum of Philadelphia, 1895.

———. *Atlas of the City of Philadelphia, 1910*. Philadelphia: G.W. Bromley & Co. Anthanaeum of Philadelphia, 1910.

"West Philadelphia." *Wikipedia*. http://en.*Wikipedia*.org/wiki/West_Philadelphia. Accessed 30 April 2012.

"Wilbur Chocolate Company." *Wikipedia*. http://
en.*Wikipedia*.org/wiki/Wilbur_Chocolate_Company.
Accessed 30 April 2012.

"Wildwood, New Jersey." *Wikipedia*. http://en.*Wikipedia*.
org/wiki/Wildwood,_New_Jersey. Accessed 30 April
2012.

"William Cramp and Sons." *Wikipedia*. http://
en.*Wikipedia*.org/wiki/William_Cramp_and_Sons.
Accessed 30 April 2012.

Woodall, Peter. "Paint It Black." *Hidden City Philadelphia*.
http://hiddencityphila.org/2012/01/paint-it-black/.
Accessed 3 January 2012.

———. "Wish You Were Here." *Hidden City Philadelphia*.
http://hiddencityphila.org/2011/12/wish-you-were-here/.
Accessed 14 December 2011.

Works Progress Administration. *1942 Land Use Maps*.
Map Collection of the Free Library of Philadelphia.

———. *1962 Land Use Maps*. Map Collection of the Free
Library of Philadelphia.

"The Writing on the Wall Foundation: Historic Façade
Advertisements." Stichting Tekens Aan De Wand. http://
www.historischegevelreclames.nl. Accessed 30 April
2012.

"Wurlitzer." *Wikipedia*. http://en.*Wikipedia*.org/wiki/
Wurlitzer. Accessed 30 April 2012.

About the Author

Lawrence O'Toole is a graphic designer, design director and entrepreneur with over fifteen years of experience in branding and print and digital design. He lived within the Philadelphia city limits for thirty-five years. He was born and raised in South Philly, moved to his first apartment in Queens Village, his second apartment in Northern Liberties and eventually bought a row home in Fishtown. In 2010, he moved to Manhattan, where he currently resides.

After attending Saint Joseph's Preparatory High School, he received a degree in graphic design from the Nesbitt College of Design Arts at Drexel University. This book began as an offshoot of his Drexel University senior thesis project. The premise of the thesis was to develop a book that would document a particular environment. This space would eventually be narrowed down to a few blocks in the Olde City area of Philadelphia. The documentation would consist of found materials, archival maps and the author's own photography.

In the course of his research for the thesis, Lawrence became intrigued by the mysterious eroded signs plastered on the sides of older buildings throughout the city. He recorded these signs as photographs and set them aside for later.

Lawrence completed his senior thesis at the end of his time at Drexel and graduated with honors. He later self-published the thesis in 2002. Entitled 24687531, the book was a pure graphic observation and interpretation of space. Eventually, curiosity about the meaning and significance of these signs would germinate the inspiration for this book's more historical approach.

Since graduation, he worked as an art director at various companies in the Philadelphia area before co-founding his own agency located just north of the city in 2005. Lawrence began an attempt to photograph and document signs in earnest, originally just to capture and preserve their image before demolition, shortly after his thesis was completed. This occurred at a time when blogging was becoming an interesting way for individuals to easily post information to share with like-minded individuals on the Internet. Eventually, he began seeking out signs in order to map their locations, find out about their histories and share them with others online. He posts photographs of his findings to his blog, "The Ghost Sign Project." It was this blog that led The History Press to invite him to contribute a book as part of a series about ghost signs in American cities.

Not content with a simple blog for the project, Lawrence has developed an application for mobile devices, which, like the blog, can provide interesting backstory and historical information on signs, but it has expanded its reach beyond just Philadelphia. The application allows anyone to capture signs and submit them for inclusion in the database of signs already collected. In this way, signs around the world can be captured, preserved and shared with others.

Lawrence currently resides in Manhattan. He worked as an independent design director for the likes of Google, Interbrand, Rokkan, Euro RSCG, StrawberryFrog, the Michael J. Fox Foundation and others before assuming the role of design director at Momentum Worldwide, a leading ideas agency with expertise across the marketing spectrum. He is also a founding partner of The Working Assembly, a collective of creatives specializing in collaboration and design services for independent clients and startups.

In addition to his design interests, Lawrence is also a runner and cyclist and has started competing in half marathons and duathlons. He was an avid fencer during his high school and college years and was active in international competitions. He is also highly interested in motoring, with a love for cars that goes back to his earliest memories. Lawrence has written articles for MotoringFile, the world's leading news source on the MINI brand of automobiles. He also maintains a website dedicated to 1970–72 Yamaha 350 R5 two-strokes and similar vintage motorcycles, which has been widely regarded as the authority on the subject.

For Further Exploration

Fading Ads of Philadelphia Website
Stay up to date by signing on to our mailing list, find out about author appearances, read up on all the latest press and preview the book on the official website for *Fading Ads of Philadelphia*. Please visit us at fadingadsofphiladelphia.com.

Fading Ads of Philadelphia Facebook Page
Stay up to date with all the latest news and events about the book, the iOS app and the blog. Post your own signs, share with your friends and spread the word! Be sure to visit and like Facebook.com/FadingAdsOfPhiladelphia.

Fading Ads of Philadelphia Mailing List
To be informed about news and offers regarding the book, sign up for the *Fading Ads of Philadelphia* mailing list by sending an e-mail to signup@fadingadsofphiladelphia.com.

Ghost Sign Project Blog
This book began from content found within "The Ghost Sign Project," a blog that I have been maintaining since 1995. The blog features photographs and documents about hand-painted advertisements and ghost signs on buildings. Originally, the goal of the blog was just to capture and preserve images of old signs before demolition, but it has since evolved into mapping their locations, finding out as much as I can about their history and sharing this information with others online. Please visit ghostsignproject.com for more.

Ghost Sign Project App
Discover, share and preserve fading ads and ghost signs all over the world with "The Ghost Sign Project" application, available for iOS devices.

A city's faded painted advertisements—the ghosts of a lost urban landscape—are history in plain sight. They are tangible ways to tell the histories of changing neighborhoods, industries and ways of life. "The Ghost Sign Project" app presents a new way to view these forgotten urban stories. Locate signs near your current location. Get historical information and incredible photos for each sign. Rate and share your favorites, and contribute your own to the growing collection, all within the app!

The goal of "The Ghost Sign Project" app is to capture images of fading signage and advertisements and create an archive to document and share these images so that their memory can be preserved before they are lost altogether. Whether you are a history buff, an urban archaeologist, a designer who loves lettering or just curious, "The Ghost Sign Project" app will help you discover faded advertisements around the corner and around the world.

With "The Ghost Sign Project" app, you can:
- View full-screen photos of a growing archive of faded ads and ghost signs.
- Visually sort signs by distance from your current location.
- Rate signs and view popular signs by a ranked list.
- Share your favorite signs on Facebook, Foursquare, Twitter or e-mail.
- View detailed information about each sign, such as neighborhood, location, condition and historical background.
- Take photos of signs you discover and contribute your findings directly from the app

Ghost Sign Project Twitter Feed
Stay up to date with new fading ad findings, special announcements and news about the book, the app and the blog. Visit and follow via @ghostsign on Twitter.

Ghost Sign Project Foursquare Lists
Check out this list of signs that have been geotagged in Foursquare. Check in, comment, post a photo and share signs you find out there in the world. Find as many as possible and mark them off as done. Join Foursquare to get this list on your phone! Visit http://4sq.com/ghostsignlist for more.

Ghost Sign Project on Pinterest
Check out this collection of ghost signs that have been pinned to my board on Pinterest. Comment, share and add the signs you find out there in the world. Visit http://pinterest.com/lotoole3/ghost-signs for more.

Ghost Sign Project on Instagram
Check out this list of signs that have been hashtagged on Instagram. Post a photo, tag it with #ghostsign and share signs you find out there in the world. Download the free Instagram app to get started! Visit http://instagr.am to find out more.

Visit us at
www.historypress.net